COLONIAL REVIVAL FURNITURE
WITH PRICES

COLONIAL REVIVAL FURNITURE

WITH PRICES

DAVID P. LINDQUIST
AND CAROLINE C. WARREN

Wallace-Homestead Book Company
Radnor, Pennsylvania

Library of Congress Catalog Card No.: 92-50671
ISBN 0-87069-660-2

Complete descriptions and prices for furniture
shown on the front cover can be found
in the color section and on pages 98 and 127.

1 2 3 4 5 6 7 8 9 0   2 1 0 9 8 7 6 5 4 3.

To our parents
Chester and Ruth Lindquist
and
David and Rebecca Warren

———————

CONTENTS

ACKNOWLEDGMENTS

Many people helped us gather the information and photographs for this book. We would like to thank everyone who graciously allowed us to come into their homes and photograph their furniture in Chapel Hill, Durham, and Edenton, North Carolina. We would especially like to thank Michael Ivankovich and Ed Nadeau for contributing their time and expertise. We received invaluable information from a great many auction houses and antiques shops, which are included in the List of Contributors.

We would like to thank the following people for their advice and help: Brad Barker, John Sykes, Rebecca W. Warren, Rebecca D. Warren, Marcia Crandall, John H. Smith, Henry Lewis, Elizabeth Moore, Arch Johnson, Chris Allen, and Harry Rinker.

Many people at libraries and museums were a great help to us. We would like to thank Neville Thompson of the Winterthur Library; Gordon Olson of the Grand Rapids Public Library; Carl Voncannon of the Furniture Library, High Point, North Carolina; Michael Ettema of the Edison Institute, Dearborn, Michigan; Ulysses Dietz of the Newark Museum, New Jersey; Rodris Roth at the Smithsonian Institution; Chris Carron of the Public Museum of Grand Rapids; Kenneth Zogry of the Bennington Museum, Vermont; Thomas Michie of the Rhode Island School of Design, Providence; Diane Dunkley of the DAR Museum, Washington, D.C.; Kate Cloninger of the International Home Furnishings Center, High Point, North Carolina; and Nicholas Bragg and King Disher of Reynolda House, Museum of American Art, Winston-Salem, North Carolina.

Special thanks also go to the staff at Whitehall at the Villa Antiques and Fine Art, Chapel Hill, North Carolina, for their support.

Introduction and State of the Market

*C*olonial Revival in the context of this book is furniture made in America between 1870 and 1940 that copies seventeenth- and eighteenth-century American styles. These styles include Jacobean, William and Mary, Queen Anne, Chippendale, Hepplewhite, Sheraton, and American Empire. One may rightly protest that not all of these styles were Colonial. However, around the turn of the century, when so much Colonial Revival furniture was made, the label "Colonial" was frequently applied to Empire-style reproductions and, indeed, to all the other original styles as well. The term "Colonial" has been used loosely since the time it was coined and we use it just as freely here as the Colonial Revivalists did. Although Colonial-style reproductions are still being made today, we chose to end our coverage at 1940. The creativity of the Colonial Revival movement had reached its peak during the 1920s, and the 1930s saw few new developments in terms of style. In the 1930s Colonial Revival furniture became more predictable, often copying specific museum pieces. There were larger numbers of accurate reproductions, but the interesting developments in Colonial Revival furniture had faded by the beginning of World War II.

This ground-breaking book will be of interest to collectors not only for the compilation of photographs of the seemingly infinite variety of Colonial Revival pieces found on the market today but also for the prices attached to these pieces. Colonial Revival furniture is in the process of undergoing a rapid expansion in the antiques and decorative arts markets in the United States as it moves from flea markets, mall shows, and group or mall shops into respected antiques and decorative arts shops. Colonial Revival pieces are turning up in auctions, including the major houses in New York. Almost every auction in New York City at Sotheby's or Christie's in the last two years has contained numerous examples of Colonial Revival furniture. In addition, the number of specialists in the field is increasing, and they are concentrating their time and effort on just a few Colonial Revival furniture makers. Furthermore, we see specialists developing. One example is Michael Ivankovich, who has made a name for himself writing about and selling the work of Wallace Nutting's shop. Another is Nadeau's Auction Gallery in Windsor, Connecticut, which has annual sales featuring the work of the Nathan Margolis Shop, the work of Abraham Fineberg, and other fine shops in the Hartford, Connecticut, area from the 1920s on. Along with this mobility, of course, has come a rapid increase in value. As these pieces have become more respectable in the collecting/decorating scheme, prices have escalated.

Two qualities must be present in a Colonial Revival piece in order for it to increase rapidly in value. First, it must copy a difficult-to-find genuine period antique. Second, to reach the highest levels of value, the piece must be faithful to the original design, and it must copy designs of the finest quality from the eighteenth and early nineteenth centuries. Perfect supporting examples are found in the sections on Colonial Revival dining chairs. The reader will immediately notice striking differences in price. Those differences are clearly attributable to the rarity of authentic antiques upon which these pieces are based, as well as to the high quality of the copies. For dining tables, too, we see a considerable increase in value. Fine antique banquet tables are rarely found on the market today, and when they are found, they are excruciatingly expensive. And again, only the very finest examples of chairs or tables command the highest prices on today's market.

It seems clear that there is a high level of sophistication among both buyers and purveyors of Colonial Revival furniture. Collectors and dealers focus on faithfulness to style, quality of materials used, rarity of the originals, and the makers and their reputations both at the time of manufacture and over the decades. This latter point is extremely important because it documents the likely longevity of pieces. Pieces made to exacting standards of quality in solid wood; or of heavy, thick veneers are proving to have great durability. Collectors and dealers know the companies whose merchandise from this era has survived in fine condition. Such large companies as Paine Furniture Company of Boston, small companies such as Sypher & Company of New York City, or cabinet makers such as Potthast Brothers of Baltimore come readily to mind as highly collected makers of fine-quality pieces.

The expansion of the Colonial Revival market is nothing short of staggering. In twenty years we have seen a considerable expansion of interest in the market into what is clearly twentieth-century-manufactured Colonial Revival furniture. These pieces, which were until recently found only in yard sales, house sales, or mall shows, are now found in nearly every antiques and decorative arts shop in cities and towns across America.

This guide provides many keys to evaluating the pieces that are so changing the face of the antiques shops of America. We hope you enjoy using it.

PART I

History of Colonial Revival Furniture

1

Construction Techniques

Because Colonial Revival furniture attempts to copy the design of seventeenth- and eighteenth-century American furniture, the collector must understand first and foremost how to tell the difference between an original period piece and the nineteenth- or twentieth-century copy it inspired. In many cases, just a glance or a casual inspection will tell you that the style is not authentic and that the proportions do not replicate the original. The collector new to Colonial Revival furniture should also know something about the construction techniques of each period. We will not attempt an exhaustive discussion of construction techniques here since they have been covered so thoroughly in other books.[1] We do, however, want to provide you with some basic information that you will need as you become more familiar with Colonial Revival furniture.

In this brief guide to construction techniques, we will not discuss seventeenth-century construction apart from eighteenth-century methods. The fact is that most seventeenth-century American pieces are in museums and private collections. You will seldom find on the market a Jacobean or William and Mary piece that was made in America that is not a later

reproduction. When you do see seventeenth-century-style pieces, you *must* find real signs of age—shrinkage, warping of boards, patina, hand-saw marks, mortise and tenon joints, and the like—before even considering that it might be a period piece. Of course, when looking at seventeenth-century-style pieces, it is imperative to know seventeenth-century forms. William and Mary coffee tables, for example, were not made until the 1920s.

A piece of Colonial Revival furniture is often easy to spot because it does not copy an earlier style accurately. Sometimes one Colonial Revival piece will even combine elements from several different style periods. Proportions tend to be irregular on Colonial Revival pieces, sometimes because the maker was not familiar with earlier designs, but just as often the reason is that the piece was made to accommodate modern ceiling heights and room sizes. Colonial Revival desks are smaller; highboys and secretaries are shorter. Colonial Revival chairs, on the other hand, are often taller and narrower than eighteenth-century chairs. Colonial Revival Chippendale-style chairs seldom capture the feeling of the substantial weight found in the originals.

The differences in the tools used to

---

1. Particularly good is Nancy A. Smith's *Old Furniture: Understanding the Craftsman's Art* (New York: Dover Publications, 1990).

construct and refine furniture are also important to know. The main difference between the hand tools used in the seventeenth and eighteenth centuries and the machine tools used in the nineteenth and twentieth centuries is that the marks left by machine tools are perfectly regular, whereas the marks of hand tools are not. You will find the marks left by various saws on areas of furniture that were not meant to be seen—on the undersides of skirt aprons, on the backs of case pieces, or underneath seat rails, for example.

Figure 1–1 shows the marks left by an eighteenth-century bow saw. You will notice that the up-and-down marks are not perfectly parallel. These marks are typical of uneven hand sawing. Figure 1–2 shows the easily identifiable, sweeping marks created by a circular saw, which was not used in America until about 1830. Figure 1–3 shows band-saw marks, which are even and parallel. You will find this perfect regularity, a telltale sign of machine work, on late nineteenth- and twentieth-century furniture.

In figure 1–4, we turned over a c. 1890 Colonial Revival Chippendale-style chair to check for machine-made marks. Although the chair might confuse the novice because of its relatively good design, underneath the seat rail we found visible machine saw marks, a sure sign of a late nineteenth-century reproduction. Circular-saw marks are visible on the seat rail and band-saw marks are noticeable under the applied shell.

The underside of legs is another good place to look for saw marks. In figure 1–5 we examined a c. 1900 Colonial Revival

Fig. 1-1 Bow-saw marks.

Fig. 1-2 Circular-saw marks.

Fig. 1-3 Band-saw marks.

tea table for saw marks and found band-saw marks, which designate the table as a turn-of-the-century reproduction.

Figure 1–6 shows bow-saw marks on the inside of the apron on an eighteenth-century lowboy. The irregular marks are a clear sign of handwork. On the back of a drawer, we see the furrows or troughs of the hand plane that have worn and softened with time (figure 1–7).

Another aspect of furniture construction that helps us date a piece is the method of joinery, especially on case pieces. When you examine a case piece, always look at the dovetails on the drawers to see if they are handmade. Of course, small shops even in the twentieth century still make dovetails by hand. But even

these dovetails will not be as fine as an eighteenth-century handmade dovetail. Figure 1–8 shows fine handmade dovetails on an eighteenth-century secretary drawer. Note how small the dovetails are, how sharp the angles are, and that the spacing is not perfectly regular. Finally, note the dovetails on the c. 1930 sewing table in figure 1–9, which are obviously machine-made.

To determine the age of Colonial Revival chairs, here are several tips you will find helpful. If you look at the back of a good eighteenth-century chair, you will see that the outline of the splat has been "silhouetted" (figure 1–10). The edge of the design has been beveled so that it is thicker in front than in back. The purpose

Fig. 1-4 Underside of a c. 1890 Colonial Revival Chippendale-style seat rail showing circular-saw marks on the rail and band-saw marks on the underside of the scalloped shell.

Fig. 1-5 Underside of a c. 1900 Colonial Revival tea table showing band-saw marks on underside of legs.

Fig. 1-6 Underside of the shaped apron on an eighteenth-century lowboy. Note the irregular marks of the bow-saw.

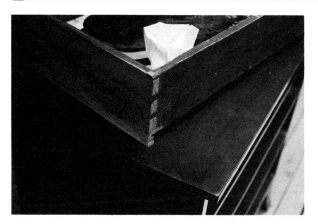

Fig. 1-7 Random hand-planing marks on the back of a drawer.

Fig. 1-8 Eighteenth-century handmade dovetails. Note the sharp angles and slight irregularity of spacing.

Fig. 1-9 Machine-made dovetails from the drawer of a c. 1930 Colonial Revival sewing table. The dovetails are small, perfectly regular, and not sharply angled.

Fig. 1-10 Back of an eighteenth-century chair showing silhouetting (or chamfering) of the splat.

of silhouetting is to maintain crisp design definition when viewed from an angle. On a chair without silhouetting, the splat will look muddy or fuzzy when viewed from an angle. Silhouetting was one extra step that the furniture maker took in making a fine eighteenth-century chair, and it was the sort of step that was omitted when making machine copies in the late nineteenth and early twentieth centuries. You will not find silhouetting on Colonial Revival chairs (see figure 1–11).

Still looking at the back of the chair, notice how the splat is attached to the shoe. As a rule, the shoe on an eighteenth-century chair will be separate from the seat rail. Look closely at the eighteenth-century chair in figure 1–12 and you will see the separate shoe. The Colonial Revival chair in figure 1–13 has an integral

Fig. 1-11 Back of a c. 1910 Colonial Revival Chippendale-style chair showing no silhouetting of the splat.

Fig. 1-12 Back of an eighteenth-century chair showing the two-part shoe.

Fig. 1-13 Back of a c. 1890 Colonial Revival chair showing an integral (one-piece) shoe.

shoe, in which the shoe and the seat rail are in one piece. This is another step that was omitted in the process of making a chair after the eighteenth century.

Next, look at the chair to see how the stretchers were joined together. Furniture makers in the eighteenth century used the mortise-and-tenon method for joining stretchers to legs. To do this by hand required great precision, and the stretcher was lined up flush with the edge of the leg to make measuring and cutting easier. The tenon was simply inserted into the mortise, a little glue was used, sometimes a peg was added (perhaps later for more strength), and that was it. In the late nineteenth century these same joints would have been produced by machine, and the stretchers will be positioned in the center of the legs rather than flush with the edge.

Figure 1–14 shows a centered stretcher on a Colonial Revival chair. Often dowels were used on Colonial Revival pieces instead of the mortise-and-tenon joint. Figure 1–15 shows a dowel joint on a Colonial Revival chair. This type of joint is not

Fig. 1-14 Centered stretcher on a c. 1890 Colonial Revival chair.

Fig. 1-15 Use of a dowel on a c. 1915 Colonial Revival chair.

as strong as the mortise-and-tenon joint, but it is simpler to implement. A dowel joint is made simply by cutting two round holes—one in the stretcher and one in the leg—and then inserting the round dowel in each hole. You can sometimes see the dowel if the joint is a little loose. You will see light through the joint, since the dowel itself is not as thick as the pieces it joins. These joints tend to loosen more easily than do mortise-and-tenon joints. Figure 1–16 shows a double dowel joint, used for extra strength, on a Colonial Revival tea table.

Weight is a dead giveaway when trying to determine the age of a piece of furniture, especially if the piece is made of mahogany. Eighteenth-century Santo Domingo mahogany is dense and heavy. If you have ever had to move eighteenth-century furniture, you know that! In contrast, a Colonial Revival chair that may have a good Chippendale look will be much lighter in weight. Why is this? The supply of Santo Domingo, Cuban, and Honduran mahogany began to diminish after 1800 and furniture makers had to turn to other geographic locations, such as South America and the Philippines, for

Fig. 1-16 Double dowel joint on a c. 1900 Colonial Revival tea table.

11

stock. The wood from each of these areas has its own characteristics. Cuban mahogany is very strong, and African mahogany has a finer texture than the wood from Mexico and the Philippines. All of these woods, however, are lighter in weight than Santo Domingo mahogany.

Not only is the wood lighter in Colonial Revival furniture, but boards were not as wide as those used in the eighteenth century. Often, an eighteenth-century tilt-top table will have a top made of only one board—or no more than two. If a table top has been made from a board less than 20″ wide, that's a good sign that it is not an eighteenth-century piece. Nineteenth-century boards tend to be thinner, as, of course, does veneer. In fact, in furniture made in the 1920s through the 1940s, you will find plywood used in drawer bottom and for the backs of case pieces.

Another thing you must know about wood is that, as it ages, it shrinks across the grain. In other words, a round table top from the eighteenth century will simply not be perfectly round today. You may not be able to see the shrinkage with the naked eye, but get out your ruler and the numbers will tell the tale. You will not find this kind of shrinkage on a Colonial Revival piece from the 1920s or 1930s, or even on a piece from the 1880s or 1890s.

Carving will tell you a great deal about the age of a piece of furniture. After you have examined many eighteenth-century pieces, as well as Colonial Revival ones, you will be able to recognize that later carving is flatter, neither as deep nor as detailed (see figure 1–17). Ball-and-claw feet will display these same characteristics. Genuine eighteenth-century American feet have strength and vitality, whereas Colonial Revival examples from the early twentieth century are more stiffly schematic, lacking the energy and grace of the originals. Some carving styles, like the roundel on the Colonial Revival lowboy in figure 1–18, are borrowed from late nineteenth-century carving styles, not from the eighteenth century.

Fig. 1-17 Hand-carved drawer front from a c. 1920 Colonial Revival highboy. The carving, though by hand, is flat and stiff, with very little undercutting, cruder than eighteenth-century carving.

Fig. 1-18 Applied roundel on a c. 1880–1900 Colonial Revival lowboy, a machine-made ornament often used on Renaissance Revival and Eastlake furniture. A roundel on a Chippendale-style piece is a clear sign of Colonial Revival decoration.

When looking at fluted or reeded carving, you can determine if it was machine-made by its perfect regularity. On handmade carving you will notice slight imperfections and irregularities. Again, this is something you will learn to recognize once you have spent time looking at actual examples.

In addition to design and construction materials and techniques, you will notice the difference in the kinds of nails and screws used in the eighteenth century as opposed to the late nineteenth and early twentieth century. This is a specialized area of study, but we can suggest a few rules. From about 1815 to 1890, machine-cut or square nails were used, and they have square heads. After 1890 you will find wire nails with round heads: this is what you will find on Colonial Revival furniture. The slots in the heads of early screws are off-center because they were made by hand. Machine-made screws will have perfectly centered slots.

Hardware offers easier clues to dating a piece. Rarely will you find original brasses even on eighteenth-century pieces because they do wear out, so this point is almost academic. On Colonial Revival pieces, the brasses have been stamped rather than cast. In the second half of the nineteenth century, they were stamped by hand, and in the twentieth century they are machine-stamped. You will see little wear or patina on Colonial Revival brasses.

This basic discussion of construction techniques will get you started as you examine Colonial Revival furniture. Learning to distinguish Colonial Revival furniture from original period antiques involves studying the history of American furniture design, along with plenty of hands-on experience with antiques, in order to become familiar with the true signs of age.

2

Colonial Revival Furniture before 1900

Important and informative articles have been published on the Colonial Revival movement, and we will synthesize information from these sources here as it applies to furniture. Late nineteenth-century trade catalogues, manuscripts, and contemporary accounts of nineteenth century exhibitions and fairs that sometimes featured antiques have all been used as source material for this history.

One of the subjects we explored in doing our research for this book was the misleading term "Centennial," which is often applied to early Colonial Revival furniture. Antiques dealers, auctioneers, and collectors often use the term to add cachet to a Colonial Revival piece. "Centennial," used loosely at best, carries the connotation of a good-quality piece from around the time of the United States Centennial, the year 1876, that makes attractive use of eighteenth-century American design elements. The use of this term might lead one to think that Colonial designs were popular at the Centennial Exhibition, held in Philadelphia. This is simply not true, however. Rodris Roth and Kenneth Ames have shown that practically no Colonial-style furniture was on display at the Centennial Exhibition. What was marketed at the Centennial was Renaissance Revival, Rococo Revival, Eastlake, Neo-Grec (a term used in the

1870s to describe a subset of Renaissance Revival style which incorporated Egyptian and Greek motifs in a somewhat fanciful way), and patent furniture. It would be more accurate to call these styles "Centennial" than to apply that term to Colonial Revival furniture.

Why not abandon the label "Centennial" altogether? We suspect that dealers and collectors like the term because it signifies the beginnings of the movement, and of course everyone tends to think the earlier, the better. But with Colonial Revival furniture, *earlier* is not necessarily *better.* The best pieces produced throughout the Colonial Revival period tended to be made in small shops by workers who either had access to originals to study and copy or who had benefited from some of the scholarship on American antiques published during the 1890s. A few small shops were making fairly faithful copies of Colonial designs in the 1880s and 1890s: for example, Meier and Hagen as well as Sypher & Company of New York City, and Potthast Brothers in Baltimore. However, small shops were also making good handmade reproductions in the 1920s and 1930s, such as Margolis of Hartford, Connecticut, and Wallace Nutting of Framingham, Massachusetts. Soon after the Centennial some inaccurate (read *ugly*) Colonial designs were also being sold. Paine Furniture Company of Boston,

Wanamaker's of Philadelphia, and several Grand Rapids, Michigan, companies produced more than a few hideous pieces. So, simply because a piece was made near the time of the Centennial Exhibition is no guarantee of quality. Rather than an early date, what you want to look for is (1) good design, (2) good materials, and (3) high-quality workmanship. We can find all these elements in the 1880s and also in the 1920s and 1930s.

In the middle of the nineteenth century, the popular furniture styles in America were Renaissance Revival, Rococo Revival, and Eastlake. At the same time, a small segment of the population began to take an interest in antique furniture. This interest first manifested itself in *collecting* and reclaiming family heirlooms from the attic or barn—or in coercing unsophisticated neighbors to give up an old table or two from their garage. Only as antiques became more popular did reproductions begin to appear in order to meet public demand for the tastes of the past.

Christopher Monkhouse and Thomas Michie have documented the earliest beginnings of the Colonial Revival movement, evident in the nation's first local bicentennial celebrations. Plymouth, Massachusetts, had its Bicentennial in 1820, and Providence, Rhode Island followed in 1836.[1] In the 1840s antiques were the rage in towns or cities such as Providence and to a lesser extent, Boston. Then, as ever, it was common to exaggerate the merits of the provenance of a piece. An article from a Providence newspaper from the 1840s mocked the huge quantities of furniture reportedly brought over on the Mayflower.[2] Even as early as the 1840s, reproductions were being made, but the evidence suggests that the numbers were far smaller than those later produced in the 1880s and after. In the 1840s Daniel Wadsworth had copies made of a seventeenth-century chair to give to the Connecticut Historical Society and the Wadsworth Atheneum. The copies were made by Smith Ely of New York City, and one chair is now at Pendleton House in Providence.[3] These were early signs of the movement that would be felt strongly in the rest of the country around the time of the nation's Centennial, held in Philadelphia in 1876. Providence and Boston were ahead of their time in celebrating the past.

Turning to the past became a theme in other fine and decorative arts as well and in literature, too. Nathaniel Hawthorne used a seventeenth-century New England chair as the focus for his historical narrative about Puritan New England, *Grandfather's Chair,* published in 1841. In 1843, Henry Wadsworth Longfellow published his poem "The Old Clock on the Stairs," which featured what was called in the eighteenth century a longcase clock. Subsequently it came to be known as a grandfather clock. In 1868 the artist Edward Lamson Henry used the same title as Longfellow's poem for one of his paintings. The painting was displayed at the Centennial Exhibition and undoubtedly increased the demand for the grandfather clock, which became an essential piece of furniture in a Colonial Revival home.[4]

One kind of celebration that put antiques before the general public was the Colonial Kitchen exhibit, which was a part of fund-raising fairs for the U.S. Sanitary Commission, a precursor of the Red Cross, for the Union army. Colonial Kitchens were part of the Sanitary Fairs at

---

1. Christopher P. Monkhouse and Thomas S. Michie, *American Furniture in Pendleton House* (Providence: Museum of Art, Rhode Island School of Design, 1986, 188.

2. Ibid., 10.

3. Ibid., 188–89.

4. Ibid., 11, 13, 15.

Brooklyn, Poughkeepsie, New York City, Saint Louis, Philadelphia, and Indianapolis during the Civil War. Women organized sanitary fairs featuring Colonial kitchens furnished with antique furniture. Meals were served by costumed waitresses serving Colonial fare.[5] Most kitchens included candlesticks on the mantel, a gun over the mantel, a tall clock, often a cupboard, table, chairs, and spinning wheels. These often were antiques, and sometimes there was even a "Mayflower" relic. An advertisement for the Colonial Kitchen at the 1864 Poughkeepsie Fair described it as follows: "Completely furnished as in that olden time, and the House-keeping carried on by Ladies in Costume, such as our great-grandmothers wore. Flax and wool spinning wheels in operation. Tea in the ancient style every evening from 5 to 10 o'clock."[6]

By the 1870s "antiquing" was gaining in popularity. In the 1870s *Harper's New Monthly Magazine* published many articles about the country's early days and ran features on the Colonial towns of Cape Cod, commenting on the popular pursuit of antiques.[7] When Irving Whitall Lyon published his ground-breaking book, *The Colonial Furniture of New England,* in 1891, he explained that he began collecting furniture in 1877 around Hartford, Connecticut, and that many others were doing the same.

The Centennial Exhibition of 1876

At the time of the Centennial Exhibition in 1876, New Englanders certainly had cultivated an interest in antiques, but that interest was still focused almost exclusively on the real thing, not on new reproductions. At the Centennial Exhibition itself, the great majority of the displays showcased the industrial might and ingenuity of American manufacturers, rather than promoting nostalgia for the past. Renaissance Revival and Eastlake were popular styles at the Centennial, along with patent furniture, innovative designs combining two pieces of furniture into one, or that folded into smaller spaces, such as the fold-down Renaissance Revival bed in figure 2–1; Colonial styles were not to be found for sale by American manufacturers. There were more than 2,000 exhibits featuring products of American manufacturers, and about 130 of these were furniture manufacturers. Kenneth Ames points out that holding the Centennial Exhibition in Philadelphia naturally skewed the geographic selection of manufacturers, bringing proportionately greater numbers of exhibitors from the East Coast, especially from Philadelphia and New York. About fifty furniture exhibitors were from Philadelphia, and thirty were from New York. Only eighteen exhibitors were from the Midwest, although that region certainly contained several important furniture-making centers. Five exhibitors were from Grand Rapids, Michigan, and as we shall see later Grand Rapids made the most of its exposure at the Centennial.[8]

---

5. Rodris Roth, "The New England, or 'Olde Tyme,' Kitchen Exhibit at Nineteenth-Century Fairs," in Alan Axelrod, ed., *The Colonial Revival in America* (New York: W. W. Norton, 1985), 160–71.

6. Ibid., 161, 164.

7. Rodris Roth, "The Colonial Revival and Centennial Furniture," *Art Quarterly* 27, no. 1 (1964): 64, 49.

8. Kenneth L. Ames, "Grand Rapids Furniture at the Time of the Centennial," *Winterthur Portfolio* 10 (1975): 23–24.

Fig. 2-1 Patent folding bed displayed at the Centennial Exhibition of 1876 in Philadelphia. From James McCabe's *The Illustrated History of the Centennial Exhibition* (Philadelphia: National Publishing Company, 1876).

A few antiques were displayed as part of noncommercial exhibits. An exhibit in the United States Government Building, for example, displayed some of the personal effects of George Washington, along with what was called the "Washington Elm Chair." The chair obviously had not been made during George Washington's lifetime, and it was Renaissance Revival in style. Indeed, it was especially made for the Centennial! The only furniture exhibitor who had any pieces that might be called Colonial was George J. Henkel of Philadelphia. His exhibit boasted a "set of chamber furniture in the style of 1776, made from the wood of an old maple tree that grew in Independence Square, and

was over two hundred years old." Although we do not have any pictures of the Henkel furniture, contemporary accounts suggest that it was probably like the George Washington elm chair and Renaissance Revival in style.[9]

The Centennial exhibit of the Grand Rapids firm of Nelson, Matter and Company represented that era's tribute to the spirit of 1776, which was not an emulation of eighteenth-century design at all but rather an attempt to incorporate the heroic stature of the Founding Fathers in the context of the monumental—and then popular—Renaissance Revival style. The company pulled out all the stops for the exhibit and created a massive Renaissance Revival bedstead and dresser, both decorated with niches holding full-body statues of American patriots—George Washington, Thomas Jefferson, and Benjamin Franklin. Each piece was topped with a carved American eagle (fig. 2–2).[10]

So of the American exhibits at the Centennial, the furniture that tried to commemorate the nation's early days—the Washington elm chair, the Henkel furniture, the Nelson and Matter bed and dresser—did so in the Renaissance Revival style, not in Colonial styles.

The visitor at the Centennial Exhibition could find antique furniture on display at "The New England Log House and Modern Kitchen," which was set up to provide food for Centennial-goers. There visitors could see a spinning wheel, a two-hundred-year-old chest of drawers, and other pieces of seventeenth-century American furniture associated with the Pilgrims.[11] This popular exhibit was patterned after the Sanitary Fair Colonial Kitchens and featured the same kinds of artifacts.

Although American manufacturers did not display eighteenth-century de-

9. Roth, "The Colonial Revival and Centennial Furniture," 63.

10. Ames, "Grand Rapids Furniture," 31.

11. Roth, "The Colonial Revival and Centennial Furniture," 60.

Fig. 2-2 Nelson, Matter and Company display at the Centennial Exhibition of 1876 in Philadelphia. Massive Renaissance Revival–style bedstead and dresser, with niches holding full-body statues of patriots, including George Washington. *Collections of the Public Museum of Grand Rapids.*

signs at the Centennial, there were several English furniture manufacturers that featured Queen Anne–style and Jacobean-style furniture and eighteenth-century furniture.[12]

One of the few examples we have found of "Centennial" furniture from the 1870s comes from a toy catalogue from C. W. F. Dare of New York City dated 1878, which included two examples of toy chairs inspired by the Centennial.[13] Both are fairly simple ladder-back chairs with a Pilgrim Century look. (*Pilgrim Century* style refers to furniture of the first century that European settlers were in America; this seventeenth-century furni-

ture is sturdy and simple, with turned posts and spindles.) The description for one chair calls it both "Centennial style" and "style of 1776." The other chair, a "Toy chair of 1776," is a good example of what the term "Centennial" meant in the 1870s: it was not literally the copying of styles from 1776 but simply adapting an early American style, here from the Pilgrim century. Early reproductions were often at odds with historical accuracy.

Toward the end of the 1870s we do find some evidence that reproductions were being produced. In Providence, Rhode Island, fine-quality reproductions were being made by Charles Dowler, Wil-

---

12. Monkhouse and Michie, *American Furniture in Pendleton House,* 197.

13. We would like to thank Neville Thompson, Librarian-in-Charge at the Winterthur Library, for bringing this catalogue to our attention.

liam Morlock (who formed the firm Morlock and Bayer, 1877–1908), and Rudolph Breitenstein. All of these men were fine carvers who had emigrated from England and Germany to the United States, and who put their skills to use in making interior woodwork and furniture.[14] In England, the work of Thomas Chippendale (1718–79) had never lost favor, and his styles from the mid-eighteenth century were reproduced in England as early as the 1830s. Woodworkers coming from England obviously would have been familiar with eighteenth-century furniture design.[15]

Interior Decoration: A New Simplicity

In 1878 Clarence Cook published his influential book, *The House Beautiful,* in which he advocated decorating with antiques, or, for those who did not own family heirlooms or antiques, with reproductions. Although Cook acknowledged the value of family provenance, he also admitted, "But everybody can't have a grandfather, nor things that came over on the 'Mayflower,' and those of us who have not drawn these prizes in life's lottery must do the best we can under the circumstances."[16] Cook espoused one of the central tenets of the Colonial Revival movement—that one's environment had the power to shape character. Antiques and reproductions, associated with a braver and simpler time, might inspire the same qualities in modern Americans.

The House Beautiful is full of illustrations showing how to decorate by combining antique furniture and reproductions. Cook even recommends a few firms as sources of good reproduction furniture—

for example, Cottier and Company of Boston. Cook writes, "The Messrs. Cottier long since found themselves obliged to give up importing furniture from England, as all the pieces that came from over seas had to be overhauled before they had been many weeks in this country. The chair shown in cut No. 22 [a Chippendale-style corner chair] is not a modern one, but the Cottiers have used it, or one like it, as a model, and have produced a design that takes the eye of every one who sees it."[17]

In the 1870s architects began designing Colonial Revival pieces for their Colonial Revival homes. George Fletcher Babb of New York was one.[18] Many of the architects of Colonial Revival homes must have had a hand in designing furniture as well. Another influential architect who also designed furniture was Arthur Little, who used English Chippendale designs as the basis for a set of dining chairs for a house in Boston's Back Bay in 1899.[19]

---

14. Monkhouse and Michie, *American Furniture in Pendleton House,* 23, 24.

15. Ibid., 22.

16. Clarence Cook, *The House Beautiful* (New York: Scribner, Armstrong and Company, 1878), 162, quoted in Elizabeth Stillinger, *The Antiquers* (New York: Alfred A. Knopf, 1980). 58.

17. Ibid., 71.

18. William B. Rhoads, *The Colonial Revival* (New York: Garland Publishing, 1977), 358.

19. Bainbridge Bunting, *House of Boston's Back Bay* (Cambridge: The Belknap Press of Harvard University, 1975), 41.

Furniture Makers in New York City

In the early 1880s Sypher & Company of New York City (a firm that dates back to the 1840s) was making fine reproductions. The chair in figure 2–3 is faithful in spirit to the Philadelphia Chippendale style. Obadiah Sypher made no apologies for making and selling reproductions, as he stated in an 1887 article: "My strict prin-ciple is to sell goods for what they are, copies if they are copies, originals when I am lucky enough to find any. But good, faithful, honest copies are of such worth in the market that they do not need being presented, and passed for what they are not."[20] This is certainly true of the chair pictured, which, barring close scrutiny, would pass as an eighteenth-century chair.

Sypher & Company published a pamphlet in 1885 entitled "The House-keeper's Quest: Where to Find Pretty Things" to advertise its interior decoration using both antique and modern styles. The pamphlet included numerous illustrations of antique china, silver, and pieces of furniture from Europe. "The Housekeeper's Quest" also comments on Sypher's reproductions, praising the "old colonial days" as a time when furniture "gave an air of refinement" to a home:

Such were the chests of drawers, the knee-hole tables, the high-backed chairs, the claw-foot tables and light stands, the eight-day clocks, which are again becoming familiar sights, since the renewal of old fashions has not only brought the genuine pieces out of their obscurity, but, the demand being much greater than could be supplied by the real thing, has led to the making of copies. The Messrs. Sypher & Co. produce copies of these old pieces which are in every way as handsome and well made as the originals, and so far as interior finish is concerned, their copies are often much better than their models.[21]

Take particular note of the last part of this statement: when assessing hundred-year-old items and two-hundred-year-old pieces, this distinction can be vital to sep-

Fig. 2-3 Sypher & Company (New York City) 1880–83 Chippendale-style armchair in the Philadelphia taste. Shell-and-tassel carved crest rail, gothic splat, fluted stiles, shell-carved seat rail, acanthus-carved cabriole legs with ball-and-claw feet. Rear stump legs. Mahogany, with pine slip seat. This chair actually combines disparate Philadelphia design elements that would not have been found together on one eighteenth-century chair. 29¾" wide × 24" deep × 41" high. *Museum of Art, Rhode Island School of Design, Providence. Gift of Commander William Davis Miller.* **$1,500–2,400.**

20. "Bric-a-Brac," *The Curio* 1, no. 2 (October 1887): 192. Quoted in Monkhouse and Michie, *American Furniture in Pendleton House,* 197, 198.

21. Sypher & Company, "The Housekeeper's Quest: Where to Find Pretty Things," New York, 1885, 3–4. Courtesy of The Winterthur Library.

arating the real from the hundred-year-old copy.

In the 1880s in New York City, the firm of Meier and Hagen was making reproductions as well as doing restoration work and buying antiques. Ernst Hagen's career reflected the trends in furniture making in the late nineteenth century. Hagen had been an apprentice under Duncan Phyfe and was one of the first persons to study his life. Hagen's notes tell about the difficulties of running a small shop at a time when competition from midwestern factories was becoming more intense. After 1867, he wrote, many smaller cabinetmakers were wiped out, or they found employment doing repair work for the larger concerns. Hagen was fortunate enough to survive, and his firm established private trade with some of New York's wealthy families.[22] In 1885 Louis Tiffany ordered "10 Maple Dining Chairs," ladder-back chairs with a high-arched crest,[23] a Colonial Revival interpretation of a Pilgrim Century chair. In the 1890s Meier and Hagen continued to produce high-quality reproductions, which are still desirable today. Since Hagen had been an ardent student of Duncan Phyfe, many of his reproductions copy the designs of Phyfe.

Another cabinetmaker in New York City in the 1890s was R. J. Horner, who made Colonial Revival pieces as well as English reproductions into the twentieth century (see page 142).

Furniture Makers in Baltimore, Philadelphia and Boston

Baltimore in the 1880s was another furniture-making center where Colonial Revival reproductions were being made. Henry W. Jenkins & Sons, founded in 1799, made high-quality furniture, including some faithful reproductions. The company did not attempt to compete with mass-produced, machine-made furniture.[24] An 1898 publication described the firm:

Half a hundred expert upholsterers and furniture workmen are employed, and all of the resources, facilities, energies, and equipment of the establishment are devoted to the production of the finest grades of furniture and upholstering possible to American designers and
American skilled workmanship. The business of the house is conducted upon a retail basis, and is largely local, with all the leading families in Maryland, and all over the country. . . . Henry W. Jenkins & Sons takes charge of the entire job, making the necessary sub-contracts and assuming the responsibility from start to finish.[25]

A drawing from about 1880 shows "a 3'6″ Sofa in Silk Plush—Like in Sheraton's book," the design indeed being faithful to Sheraton's.[26] An undated drawing from the Jenkins archives shows a Hepplewhite *demi-lune* (or halfmoon) table of very good proportions and style with bellflower inlay. These pieces were expen-

22. Elizabeth A. Ingerman, "Personal Experiences of an Old New York Cabinetmaker," *The Magazine Antiques*, November 1963, 580.

23. Elizabeth Stillinger, *The Antiquers* (New York: Alfred A. Knopf, 1980), 54.

24. John H. Hill, "Furniture Designs of Henry W. Jenkins & Sons Co." *Winterthur Portfolio* 5 (1969): 162.

25. *Baltimore 1898,* compiled by the Mercantile Advancement Company of Baltimore (Baltimore: The Company, 1898), 181. Quoted in Hill, "Furniture Designs of Henry W. Jenkins & Sons Co.," 163.

26. Hill, "Furniture Designs of Henry W. Jenkins & Sons Co.," 180.

sive, with Jenkins charging for a Hepple-white secretary-bookcase "without lid & no inlaying $115.00, without lid & with inlaying $135.00, with lid and with inlay $150.00."[27]

Also working in Baltimore in the 1880s was C. F. Meislahn & Company. Part of its output is a chair that reminds us that Colonial Revival furniture often added on to eighteenth-century designs: Figure 2–4 shows a Chippendale-style rocking chair with ball-and-claw feet and, yes, rockers! This is not a design that we take seriously today, but it demonstrates that the Colonial Revival movement certainly was not tethered to slavish copies.

Philadelphia's furniture makers were also engaged in making reproductions. According to *The Decorator and Furnisher,* August Wunsch was making reproductions in the 1880s. No doubt there were other small cabinetmakers as well. In the last quarter of the nineteenth century, Philadelphia still had many small cabinetmaking shops of one or two skilled craftsmen producing good-quality reproductions.

Beyond the small cabinetmaking firms, larger companies such as Wanamaker's of Philadelphia also sold Colonial Revival furniture in the 1880s. One of Wanamaker's catalogues from around 1887 advertised a "Dining Room in Colonial style," which although mostly heavy golden oak, did include dining chairs in a quasi-Chippendale style with rather elongated gothic-inspired splats, cabriole front legs, and paw feet, available in oak or mahogany. The same catalogue also featured a chair with a gothic-inspired splat, tufted seat, and straight legs.[28]

Paine Furniture Company was one of the largest furniture manufacturers in Boston, and it was producing Colonial Revival furniture, along with other styles, in the 1880s. One of its catalogues from the

Fig. 2-4 C. F. Meislahn & Company (Baltimore) c. 1880 mahogany Chippendale-style rocking chair— an imaginative adaptation of Chippendale. *Copyright © Smithsonian Institution. Courtesy Paul Mason.* **$800–1,200.**

end of that decade shows a number of "colonial desks"—slant-front desks, some with galleried tops, most with some carving on the slant front and/or drawers, and bracket feet, available in cherry, oak, or mahogany. Paine Furniture Company's 1890 catalogue, "Suggestions to Those Who Would Furnish," contains several illustrations of Colonial Revival furniture, along with advice on how to decorate the home by avoiding excessive ornament and instead striving for grace and simplicity. The catalogue shows a "Colonial Desk Chair," a Chippendale chair with straight legs, and a "Colonial Desk," a broadly carved, blocked slant-front desk with quarter-columns on bracket feet. Also illustrated is a "Colonial Sideboard," which owes more inspiration to Empire than to Chippendale, with a heavy backsplash incorporating beveled glass

27. Ibid., 181.
28. "Wanamaker's Furniture," c. 1887, 155, 189, 135. Courtesy of The Winterthur Library.

and scrolling brass. The dining chairs in the same illustration are Chippendale in style. The dining-room chair in figure 2–5 was made by Paine Furniture Company around 1890.

Paine's summer catalogue from 1897 includes Windsor chairs, accompanied by a whimsical explanation of their origin: "When George II was hunting one day in Windsor Forest he was overtaken by a storm, and took refuge in a shepherd's hut. He was surprised to find there one of the most luxurious chairs he had ever oc-cupied, and upon inquiry it was found that the shepherd had made it himself, largely with his pocket-knife. The king purchased it, and had duplicates promptly made. This is the chair. It has been known ever since as the Windsor chair."[29] This kind of narrative, associating a prestigious historical figure with a piece of furniture, was a popular sales device for Colonial Revival furniture.

In the 1880s Goldthwait Brothers and Bancroft and Dyer in Boston made fine furniture for the upper-middle class.[30] For this top-of-the-line furniture, designers were becoming important. George Clark was a trained architect who designed his own furniture for George Clarke & Company, which also provided complete decorating advice.[31] Conant, Ball and Company produced chairs in Gardner, Massachusetts, and sold them in Boston. In general, Boston furniture manufacturers around 1880 did not try to compete with the larger midwestern factories, and they relied more on word of mouth than on advertising. Many shops were relatively small and maintained traditional woodworking techniques.[32]

An interesting furniture concept from the 1880s is the spinning-wheel rocking chair (see figure 2–6), which appears to have been made in Boston and other parts of New England. These chairs embody several aspects of the Colonial Revival movement: a romanticization of the hearth and home and the roles played there by women, a glorification of hand-made items as opposed to machine-made goods, and the use of older design elements in new context—not always such a practical idea!

As Christopher Monkhouse has pointed out, the spinning wheel became

Fig. 2-5 Paine Furniture Company (Boston) c. 1890 mahogany dining chair in the Chippendale style, with gothic splat, slip seat, front cabriole legs with ball-and-claw feet, rear stump legs. Labeled. 23⅛″ wide × 19″ deep × 40½″ high. *Collection of Dr. and Mrs. Bernard Carroll.* Side chair **$400–600.** Armchair **$700–1,000.** Set of six **$4,000–6,000.**

29. Courtesy of The Winterthur Library.

30. Edward S. Cooke, "The Boston Furniture Industry in 1880," *Old-Time New England* 70 (Winter 1980): 86.

31. Ibid., 89.

32. Ibid., 93.

poem "The Courtship of Miles Standish," published in 1858, did much to popularize the spinning wheel. In the poem, John Alden is sent to propose to Priscilla Mullins on behalf of his friend, Captain Miles Standish. The courtship takes place while Priscilla works at her spinning wheel. The spinning wheel also became the subject of several nineteenth-century paintings.[34]

William B. Savage of Boston capitalized on the popularity of old spinning wheels by remaking old, broken spinning wheels into rather odd-looking chairs, which he advertised in *The Decorator and Furnisher* in 1886–87. The advertisement alluded to Longfellow's poem, quoting: "So as she sat at her wheel one afternoon in the autumn / Alden, who opposite sat, and was watching her dexterous fingers / As if the thread she was spinning were that of his life and his fortune . . ." Not surprisingly, the chair was advertised as a good wedding present.[35]

In the 1880s we see Colonial Revival furniture being produced by some of the larger companies in the East and also some good pieces being produced by small firms in the major cities on the East Coast. The 1890s continues the trend in both directions. Some good pieces were advertised by Daniels, Badger & Company of Boston. Its 1890 catalogue, "How to Furnish Our Homes," contained mostly pieces in golden oak, but it also featured a shield-back Hepplewhite chair of good proportions, called a "reception chair," which was available in cherry and mahogany as well as oak. Also advertised were parlor desks with galleried tops, slant fronts, and ogee bracket feet, all with some carving. The catalogue also offered decorating advice, which shows a reac-

one of the central artifacts of the Colonial Revival movement.[33] As New England towns began to celebrate their bicentennials early in the nineteenth century, a few relics were usually brought out for display, and spinning wheels were particularly important.

Henry Wadsworth Longfellow's

33. Christopher Monkhouse, "The Spinning Wheel as Artifact, Symbol, and Source of Design," in Kenneth Ames, *Victorian Furniture* (Philadelphia: Victorian Society of America, 1983), 159.

34. Ibid., 157, 159.

35. Ibid., 163.

tion against Victorian clutter. Grotesque ornament, an overabundance of curving lines, and suffocating Victorian bric-a-brac were now frowned upon. The author instead praises the virtues of the early days of New England, when interiors featured European and Chinese porcelains, and furniture with simpler lines.

In 1893 the World's Columbian Exhibition was held in Chicago to celebrate the 400th anniversary of Columbus's discovery of America. Like the Centennial Exhibition of 1876, this world's fair showcased the industrial might of many nations. Colonial Revival architecture was much in evidence, particularly in the group of state buildings, many of which incorporated Colonial design elements. The most recognizable building was a replica of Mount Vernon. Included in these state houses were displays of colonial relics—documents, furniture, and often anything having to do with George Washington.

Many of the furnishings for these houses were actual antiques. Other pieces were made especially for the exhibits. However, the makers of these reproduction pieces were rarely mentioned.[36] Although antiques and reproduction Colonial Revival furniture were included in the historic exhibits, Colonial Revival furniture was not being exhibited by furniture manufacturers; neither was it being displayed for purchase by the general public.[37] The importance of the Columbian Exhibition to the Colonial Revival movement lies in the fact that more than twenty million people visited the fair with its exhibits of Colonial architecture and interiors. Furthermore, what had previously been an eastern-seaboard movement now had a chance to spread to the heartland of the nation.[38] Certainly the fair must have influenced the "Colonial" designs that midwestern factories soon began to produce.

Furniture Makers in Chicago

According to Sharon Darling, who has written extensively about the Chicago furniture industry, during the 1890s several small cabinetmaking shops were producing good-quality reproductions. John A. Colby & Sons, one of Chicago's oldest furniture retailers, had been making Colonial Revival furniture as early as 1894, and by the turn of the century its factory employed one hundred workers. During the 1890s Colby produced custom-made interior woodwork, along with custom-made furniture, a popular combination in the late nineteenth century, as we have

seen in eastern cities. By 1900 designer William F. Halstrick was selling hand-made reproductions of antique Dutch chairs, and the Storey Furniture Company offered a Windsor armchair that claimed to be "a faithful reproduction of one the Mayflower patterns."[39]

In 1899 William Kennett Cowan opened a showroom for his Empire-style furniture and copies of eighteenth-century American furniture of solid mahogany and walnut. His output included such popular items as George Washington's desk (modeled after a desk that Washing-

36. Susan Prendergast Schoelwer, "Curious Relics and Quaint Scenes: The Colonial Revival at Chicago's Great Fair," in Alan Axelrod, ed., *The Colonial Revival in America* (New York: W. W. Norton, 1985), 193.

37. Roth, "The Colonial Revival and Centennial Furniture," 75.

38. Schoelwer, "Curious Relics and Quaint Scenes," 32.

39. Sharon Darling, *Chicago Furniture: Art, Craft, and Industry, 1833–1983* (New York: W. W. Norton, 1984), 203.

ton had used in New York City) and Martha Washington's sewing table.[40]

Beginning in the 1890s, department stores such as Marshall Field & Company created their own cabinetmaking shops to make reproductions. Marshall Field & Company also bought large quantities of furniture from midwestern factories.[41]

An article in the *Furniture Worker* in 1900 notes that Chicago probably had five thousand craftsmen working as woodcarvers for furniture factories. Some probably also worked for firms making mantels and millwork or in shops that specialized in carving. Many of these craftsmen had been trained in Europe.[42]

Bench-Made Reproductions

According to Gregory R. Weidman in his *Furniture in Maryland, 1740–1940*, in the last years of the nineteenth century the furniture industry in Baltimore showed many of the same characteristics seen in other eastern cities as they absorbed the competition of mass-produced furniture from midwestern factories. Weidman credits the decline in the number of furniture manufacturers and cabinetmakers to several causes in addition to competition from midwestern factories, including larger firms squeezing out smaller firms and the trend toward eclecticism in interior design. Large department stores edged out small furniture stores by selling a wide array of household furnishings to the public. On top of that, several midwestern factories had retail stores in Baltimore, so competition was fierce. One could also buy furniture through interior decorators, who bought from a variety of sources and sometimes had furniture made to order.[43]

By 1900, as the antiques trend continued, eighteen Baltimore furniture dealers had begun selling antiques. As the market for antiques grew in Baltimore, so did the manufacture of reproductions. As noted earlier, beginning in the 1870s, fine reproductions were produced by Henry W. Jenkins & Sons. By the 1890s, a number of firms were making what was called "artistic furniture," which copied the old English masters. This furniture has come to dominate the Baltimore furniture industry in this century.[44]

The most successful of these firms was Potthast Brothers, founded in 1892 by German immigrants who had been trained in woodworking techniques in Germany. Potthast Brothers specialized in fine-quality reproductions, which were popular in Maryland and the surrounding area and continue to be sought after today (see figures 2–7 and 2–8). The firm focused on dining-room furniture, often in the Hepplewhite and Empire Revival styles, and the design sources were often local, building on the tradition of Baltimore furniture design. The furniture was mostly handmade and usually was labeled. The firm proudly called its pieces "The True Antiques of Tomorrow." The firm was in business until 1975.[45]

Also in Baltimore, C. F. Meislahn & Company, founded in 1887, advertised itself as "Sculptors, designers, and manu-

40. Ibid., 210.
41. Ibid., 208.
42. Ibid., 197.
43. Gregory R. Weidman, *Furniture in Maryland, 1740–1940* (Baltimore: Maryland Historical Society, 1984), 213.
44. Ibid.
45. Ibid., 214.

Fig. 2-7 Potthast Brothers (Baltimore) c. 1903 Chippendale-style side chair in the Philadelphia manner, based on an original in a Baltimore collection. This chair is labeled "Potthast Bros/Antique Furniture/Artistic Furniture Mfrs./507 N. Howard Street, Baltimore, Maryland." Mahogany, with oak corner blocks. 24" wide × 21¾" deep × 40¼" high. *Courtesy Maryland Historical Society, Baltimore.* Single, **$600–900.** Set of six, **$6,000–9,000.** Set of eight, **$10,000–16,000.**

Fig. 2-8 Potthast Brothers (Baltimore) 1910–30 Hepplewhite Revival shield-back armchair, based on a piece in a Baltimore collection. Reeded arms and legs, spade feet. Mahogany. 23¾" wide × 20¼" deep × 36¾" high. *Courtesy Maryland Historical Society, Baltimore.* Single, **$500–750.** Pair, **$1,200–1,800.** Set of eight, **$6,000–9,000.**

facturers of plain and artistic furniture and interior work."[46] An example of Meislahn's work from about 1880 is the Chippendale-style rocking chair shown in figure 2–4. The firm was in business until 1941.

One Baltimore manufacturer that turned out reproductions and fine custom furniture around the turn of the century was J. W. Berry & Son, a company that is still in business today (see figure 2–9). Enrico Liberti opened a shop in 1930, and built an excellent reputation during the 1930s. He made reproductions for a number of public buildings, and his shop continues to make reproductions today.[47]

Figures 2–10 and 2–11 show examples of Empire Revival pieces made in Baltimore around the turn of the century. Empire pieces at that time were often called "Colonial," although the style ante-

46. Ibid.
47. Ibid.

Fig. 2-9 Chippendale Revival desk and bookcase, c. 1910–20, made by J. W. Berry & Son of Baltimore. Based on a Massachusetts prototype found in a Baltimore collection at the turn of the century. Mahogany and white pine. 44½″ wide × 25¼″ deep × 96″ high. *Courtesy Maryland Historical Society, Baltimore.* **$12,000–18,000.**

dates the Colonial era. Nevertheless, Empire-style pieces were an important part of the Colonial Revival.

Other furniture centers active in the 1890s included Cincinnati, Saint Louis, Louisville, Indianapolis, Rockford, Illinois, Williamsport and Allentown, Pennsylvania, and Columbus, Ohio. Grand Rapids, Michigan, a major furniture-making center, will be discussed in Chapter 3.

Before the nineteenth century drew to a close, books on American antiques began to appear. The first, published in 1891, was Irving Whitall Lyon's *The Colonial Furniture of New England.* Lyon's work was well researched and has stood the test of time, as opposed to other books of that vintage. Completing the research for his great work took Lyon to the homes of numerous collectors as well as to many antiques shops. In his journal of 1883 he describes a visit to a shop in Salem, Massachusetts, where he spotted new "antiques": "His Oaken chests were most all reproductions, newly carved brand new, & he so told me. The price was always about $75, & he said his customers bought these tight new pieces in preference to the old."[48]

Lyon studied furniture in England and France to try to uncover some of the roots of American furniture design. One important result of his pioneering research was that he proved that much of the seventeenth-century furniture then extant in New England had actually been made there, whereas previously most people assumed it had been imported from England.[49]

In 1895 Alvan Crocker Nye published *A Collection of Scale Drawings, Details, and Sketches of What Is Commonly Known as Colonial Furniture, Measured and Drawn from Antique Examples.* No doubt Nye's work, together with Lyon's was a great help to furniture manufacturers in their efforts to build good-quality reproductions.

By the turn of the century, the Colonial Revival movement had come of age,

---

48. I. W. Lyon, "Notes from Inventories on Old Furniture, etc.," manuscript, Winterthur No. 76 × 99.17. Quoted in Stillinger, *The Antiquers,* 73.

49. Stillinger, *The Antiquers,* 74.

Fig. 2-10 Empire Revival sofa made in Baltimore c. 1880–1910, a popular style around the turn of the century. Although this looks very much like a c. 1825 piece, the carving is flat and not as extensive as on an earlier piece, and the legs are too short. Mahogany and white pine. 93½″ long × 24½″ deep × 35⅜″ high. *Courtesy Maryland Historical Society, Baltimore.* **$750–1,250.**

Fig. 2-11 Empire Revival window seat made in Baltimore, c. 1890–1910. The heavy diagonal molding on the arms, the claw feet, and the flat carving are typical of Colonial Revival pieces rather than period Empire pieces. Mahogany, with oak. 47½″ wide × 19⅝″ deep × 27⅞″ high. *Courtesy Maryland Historical Society, Baltimore.* **$600–900.**

and reproductions were popular at all levels of society. As we have seen, good-quality reproductions were readily available from small shops, and they were becoming more plentiful from larger factories as well. In the next chapter we will discuss the production of these larger factories, focusing on the furniture industry of Grand Rapids, Michigan, which was one of the most important centers of factory production by the turn of the century.

3

Grand Rapids Furniture Makers and the Advent of Mass Production

By the turn of the century, Grand Rapids, Michigan, became one of the major producers of furniture. As in Chapter 2, there were several important centers of mass-produced furniture around the country. We chose Grand Rapids as the example to show how factory production fed the popular demand for Colonial Revival furniture. Grand Rapids was an important furniture producer even before the Colonial Revival gained momentum, so it is interesting to see how and when the furniture manufacturers responded to the popularity of Colonial styles. It is one of the ways that we can gauge the widespread popularity of the movement.

Much of the output of Grand Rapids factories was intended for the mass market and was affordable. In order to produce reasonably priced furniture and to increase profitability, factories used machines wherever possible to speed up production and cut costs. Thus, the great majority of these pieces could not be as well-made as the work of smaller cabinet-making shops where traditional woodworking techniques were still used. We will look at the sorts of machines used in large factories in Grand Rapids to under-

stand their limitations and the kind of furniture they were capable of producing.

The first Colonial styles coming out of Grand Rapids around 1890 were far from faithful copies, and many of these pieces do not succeed from an aesthetic point of view.

Factory-produced furniture from before the turn of the century is less desirable to today's buyer. However, we do see a great deal of it at flea markets and antiques malls, and we need to know how to distinguish among levels of quality. This mass-produced Colonial Revival furniture is what was available through mail order and to the average household, so it was influential in its own time if not in our own. The furniture coming out of Grand Rapids generally improved after the turn of the century and, by the 1920s, high-quality reproductions were available, along with plenty of low-end pieces for the mass market.

Grand Rapids was an ideal location for making furniture. There was the abundant supply of timber—both hardwood and softwood—and the town was located on the Grand River, which provided transportation for the raw timber as well as for the finished product. The river rapids provided water power for the sawmills and furniture factories. In addition, Grand Rapids had had railroad service since 1858 and could ship its products both to the South and the West, thus meeting the requirements of an expanding nation.

Many of the furniture companies in Grand Rapids began as millworks, making architectural pieces such as banisters, stairs, doors, and sashes. Nelson, Matter and Company began as a sawmill, then became a barrel factory, then expanded into making chairs, and by the 1870s had established itself as one of the mainstays of the Grand Rapids furniture industry. Chris Carron, Curator of History at the Public Museum of Grand Rapids, points out that many of Grand Rapids' successful furniture companies started out this way. Carron notes that Grand Rapids had already laid the foundation for mass production from its days in millworking. It was just a few short steps from processing lumber to making furniture. Companies were already established to take advantage of the water power, and they were easily able to transform water-powered mills into powering machines to mass-produce furniture.

During the 1870s Grand Rapids greatly increased its share of the nation's furniture industry. By 1880, it ranked seventh in the nation in the production of furniture.[1] In 1878 the city established its semiannual Furniture Market, through which it displayed and sold its products to retailers. This important marketing arena led not only to sales through furniture and department stores but also to contracts for large quantities of furniture to be sold through such mail-order giants as Sears Roebuck and Montgomery Ward. Of course, furniture made for the mail-order business was inexpensive, and

some companies in Grand Rapids that wished to be associated only with high-quality goods scorned the mail-order business. Grand Rapids indeed had companies that made cheap furniture, but many companies produced a great deal of good-quality furniture as well.

The three main furniture companies that were established by the 1870s and led the industry were the Berkey and Gay Company, the Phoenix Furniture Company, and Nelson, Matter and Company. In the 1870s these three companies built new factories that proved vital to their later success. The Phoenix factory covered 12,000 square feet of space, with four stories. The nearby sawmill had two veneer saws in addition to the usual saws. Wood was treated on site in dry kilns that had a capacity to hold 90,000 feet of lumber. The machines were powered by a two-hundred-horsepower steam engine fed by four boilers.[2]

The Nelson, Matter and Company factory was equally impressive, with its largest building covering 11,000 square feet. Machines for cutting, planing, and turning occupied the first floor. A Grand Rapids historian describes the layout in detail: "Two cutoff saws were used to cut the lumber into desired lengths, and four strip, or splitting, saws and a band saw aided by three planing machines cut the lumber to the proper width and thickness. Two jointers, six turning lathes, and a gauge lathe accomplished the remaining preliminary processes. The second floor had twenty machines for cutting, mortising, tenoning, grooving, moulding, boring, and scroll sawing. Cabinet work, veneering, and carving were done in the top two stories of this building."[3] The factory was laid out for maximum efficiency. Iron tracks allowed the lumber and other

1. Kenneth L. Ames, "Grand Rapids Furniture at the Time of the Centennial," *Winterthur Portfolio* 10 (1975): 25.

2. Frank Ward Ransom, *The City Built on Wood: A History of the Furniture Industry in Grand Rapids, Michigan, 1850–1950* (Ann Arbor: Edwards Bros., 1955), 32.

3. Ibid., 33.

heavy materials to move easily in and out of the building. The tracks were routed near a steam-powered elevator, so materials could be sent to upper floors efficiently. Such planning helped give Grand Rapids factories an advantage over the older companies in the East.[4]

In the 1870s Berkey and Gay Furniture Company built one of the largest factories in the country. Offices, showrooms, shipping facilities, storage space, and the finishing department were housed in a 16,500-square-foot, six-story building. Three other buildings housed the manufacturing processes. The company operated its own lumberyard and dry kiln. In 1889 Berkey and Gay built another six-story building, which allowed the company to double its production.[5]

One important asset of the Berkey and Gay factory in the 1870s was its two steam-powered elevators. Another is that the new factory had been designed to include space for a photography studio, as furniture manufacturers produced illustrated catalogues to help the companys' salespeople sell their products.[6]

With major factories up and running, the 1870s was the decade in which Grand Rapids established its national reputation in furniture making. In 1876 the three major Grand Rapids companies took part in the Centennial Exhibition in Philadelphia, and all received awards. The companies made good use of the opportunities for promotion and about the same time began to open showrooms in New York City to sell their furniture in the East. By the end of the decade, Grand Rapids was exporting furniture to Europe and South America.[7]

The furniture style produced in the 1870s was predominantly Renaissance Revival—massive pieces that could be ornamented to a greater or lesser degree depending upon the desired price range. It is difficult to determine which company made a particular piece of furniture from this period as many companies were producing a similar look.[8]

During the 1880s the Grand Rapids furniture industry continued to expand, fueled by westward migration. The Grand Rapids companies continued to update their equipment and added new machinery, while factories in the East lagged behind because their capital was tied up in old factories. In 1880 Berkey and Gay employeed 400 people, Phoenix employed 520, and Nelson, Matter and Company employed 380.[9]

Rather than using mass-production techniques, most Grand Rapids factories used the method of "batch" production. The companies would display several samples at exhibits such as their semi-annual Furniture Markets or in their showrooms and take orders from retailers. In general, furniture was not mass-produced and then warehoused as inventory to await sales. Pieces were made in batches of twenty-five or fifty or one-hundred as orders came in.

We tend to think that Grand Rapids produced relatively inexpensive furniture and relied heavily on mechanized processes, while smaller shops in the East and elsewhere maintained the old woodworking traditions, making furniture of higher quality for people of means. While this assumption is fairly accurate, it is instructive to look more closely at how machines were actually used in the furniture industry at the end of the nineteenth cen-

4. Ames, "Grand Rapids Furniture," 30.

5. Ransom, *The City Built on Wood,* 33.

6. Ames, "Grand Rapids Furniture," 28.

7. Ibid., 30.

8. Ibid., 34.

9. Ibid., 31.

tury. Grand Rapids furniture, though made in large quantities, still required handwork, especially on high-end pieces. Machines, after all, could not duplicate handwork. Machines allowed workers to take shortcuts and produce furniture more quickly, but they could not replicate hand-carving. Mechanization had the greatest impact on the methods of furniture making that were already inexpensive.[10]

Since the early nineteenth century, furniture manufacturers used circular saws for cutting boards and machines to plane and sand the boards, make mortise-and-tenon joints, and mass-produce dowels. Workers experimented with machines to cut dovetails and pins, the most successful being the rotary, or gang, dovetailer.[11] Band saws, which could cut curved forms, were in wide use by the 1880s, as were scroll saws or fretsaws.[12] Machine-powered lathes and gauge lathes were used to turn wood. Gauge lathes could turn several pieces of wood at a time, but they did not completely replace hand turning. Gauge lathes required many different settings to do anything beyond basic turnings, so they were cost-effective only when producing thousands of identically turned pieces. On a smaller scale, it was more economical to do simple turnings by hand rather than fit machines to do the turning automatically. Powered lathes were used, but they were not always automatic.[13]

Molding machines were available, but molding was often contracted out and done at mill-work houses. Shapers and routers were used on edges or, with attachments could cut fluted legs or regular, geometrical, applied ornaments such as the sunburst and fan patterns one often finds on Colonial Revival pieces from this era. The router, or edge molder, could make roundels and other geometric patterns also found on Colonial Revival pieces.[14]

The only machine that could come close to duplicating hand carving was the spindle carver, also in use by the 1880s. This machine required a highly skilled operator, who did the work freehand. And even with the spindle carver, the work had to be completed by hand. Even at the turn of the century, the Sligh Furniture Company of Grand Rapids employed forty hand carvers in its factory producing middle- and low-end products.[15] On pieces with any value, the carving was always finished by hand. While other "carving" machines were available, they could be used only on low-end furniture since the results obviously looked machine-produced.

By the late 1880s an embossing machine was in use but it was only capable of making a relief design, a shallow impression with no undercutting, and it was not used on high-quality furniture.[16] The multiple carver, capable of cutting several identical designs simultaneously, was limited to incising; using it for anything more complex was not cost-effective.[17]

Most of the woodworking machines in use at the end of the nineteenth century had limitations, one being that the end product was obviously machine made.

10. Michael J. Ettema, "Technological Innovation and Design Economics in Furniture Manufacture," *Winterthur Portfolio 16* (1981): 198, 201.

11. Ibid., 212.

12. Ibid., 213.

13. Ibid., 215.

14. Ibid., 216–18.

15. Ibid., 202.

16. Ibid.

17. Ibid., 220.

When producing Colonial Revival furniture, these machines could not duplicate the fine work or hand carving of early American craftsmen. Machines could produce only adaptations. The marks left from machine carving on lower-end pieces is one of the easy ways to spot Colonial Revival furniture. Large companies did have their own carvers, and on better pieces the carving was sometimes done by hand, but some pieces were contracted out to specialty carving works in Grand Rapids. Even when the carving was done by hand, however, it was not as deep or crisp as eighteenth-century carving. Anyone familiar with good eighteenth-century carving can easily spot most Colonial Revival–era carving.

After 1900 the finishing process was done by machine and often the hand-rubbing was eliminated. By the 1910s furniture was being spray finished, a process that offered great potential savings to furniture manufacturers. With a spray gun, two men could finish twenty-four chairs in an hour. With the brush-and-dip method, one man could finish only four chairs in an hour.[18] Hand-rubbing between each coat of finish added to the cost, and of course the number of coats increased the cost as well. On pieces that are beautifully and carefully finished, the finishing process can easily account for half of the final cost. The method of finishing is one important aspect of quality that collectors today look for. Not surprisingly, hand-finishing will always be more highly valued than machine-finishing.

In 1895, George Gay of Berkey and Gay described a furniture industry that manufactured two classes of furniture— low-end furniture for the general public and high-end furniture that was made to order and combined old traditional methods with new machine methods.[19] At the turn of the century, Grand Rapids produced large quantities of low-end furniture, but its manufacturers also produced high-quality pieces that still required a great deal of hand work.

Not only did the Grand Rapids furniture companies make efficient use of the available technology at the end of the nineteenth century, but they also understood the art of promotion. Grand Rapids had always marketed itself aggressively, and the semiannual Furniture Market was an essential marketing tool. Beyond that, the major companies advertised in the most important national magazines. For instance, Berkey and Gay advertized in *The Saturday Evening Post.* At the turn of the century, Grand Rapids also founded several trade journals, including *The Furniture Manufacturer, The Stylist, Furniture Record,* and *Good Furniture and Decoration.*

By the 1890s Grand Rapids had begun to promote itself as a "style center." Companies hired furniture designers who had been trained in London, New York, and Chicago and began producing copies of period pieces and furniture in the Arts and Crafts style. The Phoenix Furniture Company employed the services of David W. Kendall, who was a major designer of period furniture from 1895 to 1910. In his search for authentic period designs, he traveled to England to study examples.[20] Around the turn of the century, Grand Rapids became the home of the College of Furniture Designing, headed by Arthur Kirkpatrick, who designed for Berkey and Gay. Students could take classes at the school or through correspondence courses.

In addition to the three major Grand Rapids companies at the turn of the century, several other large companies were founded in the nineteenth century in

18. Ransom, *The City Built on Wood,* 61.

19. Edward S. Cooke, "The Boston Furniture Industry in 1880," *Old Time New England* 70 (Winter 1980): 85.

20. Ransom, *The City Built on Wood,* 27.

Grand Rapids and remained prominent through the 1920s. All these companies produced a good line of furniture that established their reputations. Phoenix Furniture Company, founded in 1870, was sold to Robert W. Irwin in 1911, who reorganized under the name Robert W. Irwin in 1920 and operated until 1953. Irwin specialized in high-quality paint-decorated furniture that emulated French designs, Japanese lacquer, and Chinese Chippendale. Imperial Furniture Company (fig. 3–1) was founded by E. H. Foote in 1903 and was bought by another company in 1954.

The Century Furniture Company was founded in 1900 (hence the name) and incorporated in 1905. From its inception, Century produced some fairly faithful copies of Empire pieces and other Colonial styles. In the 1920s Century offered a line of reproductions copying furniture from Knoll House in England. Century was in operation until 1942.

Luce Furniture Company was also founded in 1900 and made mid-priced furniture and many Colonial Revival pieces. Colonial Furniture Company of Zeeland, Michigan, was founded in 1899 and did not move to Grand Rapids until 1947. Colonial specialized in making clocks, but in the 1930s it also made reproductions of pieces in the Henry Ford Museum. Widdicomb and Sligh were two other prominent companies. Sligh made cheap to mid-range furniture and is still in business today, making desks and clocks.

Gustav Stickley does not fit the profile of the average Grand Rapids manufacturer, but he and his small firm of Stickley Brothers, which made Arts and Crafts furniture, did participate in the Furniture market in 1900. The Arts and Crafts movement had its origins in late nineteenth-century England and was devoted to craftsmanship and simple, purposeful designs meant to be used by all. The Arts and Crafts movement rejected furniture

Fig. 3-1 Imperial Furniture Company c. 1920 Hepplewhite-style card table with shaped flip top. Mahogany, with diamond and line inlays and satinwood center panel. Labeled. 36″ wide × 18″ deep × 28¾″ high. *Private collection.* **$800–1,200.**

that was too ornate to be practical, and furniture that was intended for the elite only. Stickley was the main popularizer of the movement in America, producing good quality, simple, sturdy, oak furniture that had the look of hand craftsmanship. Stickley's magazine, *The Craftsman* (1901–1916) promoted the ideals of the Arts and Crafts movement, with articles on household and decorative arts, as well as philosophy, economics and politics. Stickley had been influenced by the simplicity of early American furniture, and recalled that in 1886 he turned his attention to "reproducing by hand some of the simplest and best models of old Colonial, Windsor, and other plain chairs, and to a study of this period as a foundation for original work along the same lines."[21]

---

21. William B. Rhoads, *The Colonial Revival* (New York: Garland Publishing, 1977), 368.

Hepplewhite-style c. 1930 secretary. Top with brass finials, central brass eagle finial. Two faux-paned doors, above central door with eagle and shield inlay. Tambour sides and fitted interior. Below are two drawers with line inlay on square, tapered legs with brass cuffs. Rabetted drawers. 36¼″ wide × 18″ deep × 81″ high. *Courtesy Whitehall at the Villa Antiques and Fine Art, Chapel Hill, N.C.* **$2,000–3,000.**

William and Mary Revival c. 1915 small candlestand with shaped, molded top of beautiful burl veneer. Trumpet-turned legs, X-stretchers, ball feet, shaped apron (with band-saw marks). 19½″ × 19½″ × 24½″ high. *Courtesy Reynolda House, Museum of American Art, Winston-Salem, N.C.* **$225–295.**

William and Mary–style c. 1920 needlepoint bench with six whorl-carved feet, two curving, molded X-stretchers with central finials, trumpet-turned legs. Excellent style and fine upholstery. 44¼″ long × 18½″ deep × 18¼″ high. *Courtesy Reynolda House, Museum of American Art, Winston-Salem, N.C.* **$800–1,200.**

Jacobean-style c. 1920 open armchair with dramatically scrolling arms, stretcher base, block turnings. Handmade needlework back and seat, along with strong turnings, enhance this type of chair. 25¼″ wide × 21½″ deep × 44″ high. *Courtesy Reynolda House, Museum of American Art, Winston-Salem, N.C.* **$1,800–2,400.**

Opposite page: Very good quality c. 1890–1910 Chippendale-style armchair in the Philadelphia manner. Pierced, molded gothic splat. Molded and carved crest rail, shell-carved apron, acanthus-carved knees, ball-and-claw feet. Rear stump legs. Needlepoint seats. 22⅜" wide × 19" deep × 41" high. *Private collection.* Single, **$700–1,000.** Set of eight (six side chairs, two arm chairs), **$6,000–9,000.** *At right:* Side chair from the same set. 20½" wide x 17⅜" deep × 41" high. *Private collection.* Single, **$700–1,000.**

A creative c. 1920 adaptation combining tea table with wash basin or wig stand into one piece. Transitional Chippendale/Sheraton style. Mahogany. Top with floral inlay in a cartouche, edged in cross-banding. Shell-carved knees, pad feet. Rabetted drawers. 30" diameter × 30" high. *Courtesy Reynolda House, Museum of American Art, Winston-Salem, N.C.* **$300–435.**

Elizabethan Revival c. 1920 open armchair with acanthus-carved scrolling arms. Shell-, scroll-, and flower-carved seat rail and stretcher. Carving is flat and schematic. New machine tapestry. Found in oak or walnut. 26″ wide × 24″ deep × 48¼″ high. *Private collection.* **$1,800–2,400.**

Sheraton-style c. 1890–1910 sofa with turned, reeded legs and carved, straight crest rail. Doweled construction. *Courtesy Whitehall at the Villa Antiques and Fine Art, Chapel Hill, N.C.* **$2,000–2,500.**

William and Mary–style c. 1910 walnut high-back hall chair with elaborate pierced and carved back and front stretcher. Cabriole legs with hoof feet. Lovely old English needlepoint seat adds to the value of this chair. 20″ wide × 17½″ deep × 47″ high. *Courtesy Reynolda House, Museum of American Art, Winston-Salem, N.C.* **$400–600.**

Set of six c. 1880–1900 side chairs with bellflower and rosette carving done by hand. Molded and shaped crest rail. *Courtesy Whitehall at the Villa Antiques and Fine Art, Chapel Hill, N.C.* **$4,800** the set.

Chippendale-style c. 1920 highboy with two fan-carved drawers (hand-carved, but shallow). Broken-arch pediment, three flame finials. Handmade dovetails on drawers. Drawer openings cock-beaded. Acorn drop finials, shaped apron. Cabriole legs with volutes, pad feet. 40⅜″ wide × 20½″ deep × 81⅛″ high. *Courtesy Whitehall at the Villa Antiques and Fine Art, Chapel Hill, N.C.* **$2,500–3,500.**

Although we remember Stickley for his Arts and Crafts furniture, in 1914 he was also making Jacobean Revival pieces.

Stickley admired some eighteenth-century designs, but he did not approve of copying. Economic necessity alone had forced him to make reproductions. In a 1913 issue of *The Craftsman,* in which Colonial Revival furniture was discussed, he admitted that some early American designs would, in fact, harmonize with Craftsman designs. The 1915 *Craftsman* advertises Windsor chairs made by Stickley.[22]

Berkey and Gay is probably more representative of the mainstream furniture producers in Grand Rapids. It certainly was one of the most successful, and by the 1920s was employing 600 to 1000 people. Even with so large a factory, orders were still processed in batches of twenty-five or fifty or one-hundred. Berkey and Gay made some high-quality furniture but its major market was for mid-priced furniture.

Berkey and Gay's 1900 catalogue, "The Old Feeling, or the Past Revived," was based on the theme offered by Clarence Cooke in *The House Beautiful*, that one's surroundings—including furniture—influence a person's character. The Berkey and Gay catalogue is full of what it calls "antique reproductions" of earlier styles. Each illustrated piece is accompanied by an elaborate description of how the piece captures certain desired characteristics of the past. Over and over again, we are assured that environment shapes character—that furniture and interiors can strengthen moral fiber. As part of the description of the Colonial Toilet Table, a vanity with attached mirror, the writer waxes eloquent: "Who could be brought in daily association with such unassumed, impressive elegance, without being somewhat fashioned after it? As well say that the rays of a 4th of July sun could not warm your body as to say that such furniture can have no bearing on the development of refinement in character."[23]

The description of the Empire Revival sofa with scrolling arms and feet and tufted back and seat gives us an idea of why Empire Revival is associated with the Colonial era: "Here you have a glimpse of magnificent Colonial ideals. There is not a monotonous line in sight, yet the design is as simple as a child, as pure as a lily. . . . There is nothing else that can more adequately portray the pure ideas of Puritan life. . . . Can you conceive of the influence of such a piece in the home?"[24] While the writer has his historical periods confused, and a Puritan certainly never came near an Empire-style sofa, it is clear that Empire Revival represents the virtues of simplicity and purity, virtues also associated with the early American life. Writing about another Empire Revival piece—a three-drawer dresser with ogee mirror attached to rope-turned standards, with convex overhanging top drawer—he describes it as a "well-balanced pure Colonial reproduction."[25] He goes on to quote Henry Wadsworth Longfellow, often pressed into service by Colonial Revivalists: "In character, in manners, in style, in all things, / the supreme excellence is simplicity."

Capping off his praise of simplicity in furniture, the writer says: "Cheap, meaningless furniture rabble, may need a whole retinue of glued on filigree, of flimsy embellishments, but furniture of the Berkey and Gay quality needs no irrelevant decoration. . . . You can feel Puritan

---

22. Ibid., 373.

23. Berkey and Gay Furniture Company, "*The Old Feeling, or the Past Revived*" (Grand Rapids: Dickinson Bros., 1900), 5.

24. Ibid., 9, 10.

25. Ibid., 13.

chasteness running all through this class of workmanship."[26] The Puritans, often invoked, are praised for their quiet spirit and simple elegance.

Berkey and Gay's 1910 catalogue, "Character in Furniture," dispatched with the fulsome prose of the 1900 catalogue and exhibits a better understanding of historical style periods. The broad use of the term "Colonial," while not historically accurate, has now become standard. In the catalogue, "Colonial" is applied to Empire-style furniture, with its carved columns, claw feet, pineapple finials, and overall simplicity, which was highly valued. The catalogue explains that "Colonial" is in fact Empire style, an American adaptation of French styles after the War of 1812.

The catalogue is illustrated with "Colonial" characters posing amid period furniture. The styles include Louis XV and XVI, "Colonial" (what we would call Empire Revival), Sheraton, Flanders furniture (Elizabethan and Jacobean), the Flemish Renaissance, Chippendale (mainly Chinese Chippendale), and William and Mary. All are adaptations, but the writing reflects greater historical accuracy and understanding of the history of furniture design.

In the 1920s Berkey and Gay produced a limited number of an interesting table. The USS *Constitution,* which had been active in the War of 1812, was being restored in Boston Harbor. Part of the wood from the oarlock deck had to be replaced. Berkey and Gay bought the discarded wood and made it into one hundred "Old Ironsides" tables, modeled from a Wallace Nutting design, complete with carved eagles.

W. L. Kimerly's book on style, *How to Know Period Styles in Furniture,* published in 1912, helps explain how styles were perceived at the time. Kimerly sums up the common view on most nineteenth-century furniture when he described it as "furniture loaded with cheap ornament and meaningless carving. The main idea seemed to be 'how much' and not 'how good.' This was partly due to the introduction of labor-saving machinery, but more to untrained men going into the furniture business, many of them being entirely ignorant of the first principles of design."[27] Kimerly acknowledges that the term "Colonial" is broadly applied to describe furniture made well after 1776. The chapter "Early American or Colonial Furniture" shows Windsors, Louis XVI (a chair owned by George Washington), Sheraton, Empire, William and Mary, Dutch (or Queen Anne), Jacobean, Chippendale, and Duncan Phyfe. Kimerly notes that the most popular style of "modern Colonial" is derived from the Empire style.[28]

In the years immediately preceding 1900, many styles were produced in Grand Rapids, with no single one dominating the trade. The semiannual Furniture Market held in Grand Rapids may have encouraged regular shifts in styles. In the last years of the nineteenth century and the first years of the twentieth, the most popular styles in Grand Rapids included the French styles, English styles, and American Colonial styles. By 1915 Adam, Hepplewhite, and the French styles were no longer as popular. Chippendale remained popular, and William and Mary, Queen Anne, and Charles II were becoming more popular. Jacobean pieces hit their stride in the 1920s, and Colonial styles continued to gain in popularity throughout the 1920s[29]

Because so much furniture was being

26. Ibid., 14.

27. W. L. Kimerly, *How to Know Period Styles in Furniture* (Grand Rapids: Periodical Publishing Company, 1912), 131.

28. Ibid., 145.

29. Ransom, *The City Built on Wood,* 62.

produced in period styles, finishing processes became more important. Manufacturers turned to mahogany and walnut for these period pieces. Because of its superior strength, Cuban mahogany was especially preferred for legs, while African mahogany was prized for its fine texture. Honduran and Mexican mahogany were also used.[30] Walnut, more costly and scarce than mahogany, was used only for legs or as veneer on expensive high-quality pieces. Low-priced furniture was often made from white woods such as maple and birch. Gum was used as a secondary wood; when it was used as a primary wood, it was painted because it did not finish well. Cheap furniture from the 1920s was often made from gum.

Nearby, in Holland, Michigan, a major force in the furniture industry was about to be established, led by Siebe Baker. Cook and Baker started out in 1890 in Allegan, Michigan, making golden oak combination bookcases and china closets. In 1903 the name was changed to Baker and Company. Siebe Baker died in 1925 and his son, Hollis Baker, took over as president. Hollis Baker had a passion for antiques and made numerous trips to the East Coast, England, and the Continent in search of designs to reproduce.

In the 1920s Baker was eager to capitalize on the public's interest in Colonial Revival furniture. In 1922 it introduced a line of Colonial furniture and in 1923 produced a Duncan Phyfe suite, which was copied from the original at the Metropolitan Museum of Art in New York City. In 1926 Baker came out with a popular line of Pilgrim Century dining-room suites.[31] In 1927, under a new name, Baker Furniture Factories was producing complete living-room and bedroom suites. And in 1931 Baker introduced its first "Old World Collection" of Georgian mahogany furniture.[32] For the next fifteen years Baker produced many eighteenth-century reproductions in the English and French styles. In 1932 the company opened the Manor House in New York City, created to produce top-of-the-line furniture that was virtually handmade, including the dovetails and finishing work. By now, of course, it has sixty years of patination, wear and tear. The Baker Museum for Furniture Research was established in 1941 in Holland, Michigan, and it remains today a wonderful source of information for furniture lovers.

In the 1920s Grand Rapids began to lose some of its market to southern companies, who had access to cheaper labor and materials. The Depression spelled the end for many Grand Rapids companies, and by the end of the Depression Grand Rapids had relinquished its reputation as a national furniture center to High Point, North Carolina. As the public began to spend its money on new goods such as cars and radios, they seemed less willing to spend as much money on furniture. High Point now was the new center of inexpensive, mass-produced furniture.

Grand Rapids continued to be a center for furniture design and continued to make high-quality furniture, but the South now dominated in producing cheaper grades. In the 1930s Grand Rapids produced high-quality Colonial designs that included handwork, but by the 1940s its furniture industry was dominated by "contract" furniture—furniture made for offices, stadiums, theaters, schools, and other public places.

---

30. Ibid.

31. Sam Burchell, *A History of Furniture—Celebrating Baker Furniture: One Hundred Years of Fine Reproductions* (New York: Harry N. Abrams, 1991), 8.

32. Ibid., 109.

4

The Peak Years: 1900–1930

Elizabeth Stillinger has documented the growing interest in American antiques in the early twentieth century in her book *The Antiquers,* in which she describes the major museum exhibits and events that shaped the public's interest in antiques and subsequently increased the demand for Colonial Revival furniture. After the great exhibition fairs of the nineteenth century, the most influential exhibits in the early twentieth century were sponsored by museums, which now began to display American antiques. In 1909, the Hudson-Fulton Celebration at the Metropolitan Museum of Art in New York City held an exhibition of American furniture from Colonial times up to 1815. This was the most comprehensive and well-organized exhibit of American antiques to date, focusing primarily on furniture from New York and New England (the Midatlantic states and the South were not yet included). Objects were arranged by period and displayed in their proper context in rooms that traced the evolution of American furniture design. One result of these period rooms was that the public went away with concrete ideas about how to incorporate antiques—or reproductions—in their own homes.[1]

After the turn of the century, the Colonial Revival movement became widely popular in architecture and home furnishings. Architecture tended toward homogenous plans for homes that were smaller, had fewer rooms, and more open floor plans, and with an emphasis on efficiency and hygiene. This was an era that saw the rise of the interior decorator and the reliance on architects to bring the best of Colonial design elements to bear on homes designed for modern living.[2]

One can see from the furniture catalogues of this period the value placed on simplicity and the rejection of the excesses of the Victorian era. Simplicity came to stand for purity and for the simpler life of the early republic. Doing away with Victorian clutter, ornamentation and overdecoration was encouraged not only for aesthetic reasons but also as a means to promote a healthy, sanitary environment. The walls of Colonial Revivalists' houses were often painted white because white and ivory were colors associated with purity and it was also believed (incorrectly) that they were used by early Americans.

---

1. Elizabeth Stillinger, *The Antiquers* (New York: Alfred A. Knopf, 1980), 129–32.

2. Bridget May, "Progressivism and the Colonial Revival: The Modern Colonial House, 1900–1920," *Winterthur Portfolio* 26 (Summer/Autumn 1991): 108.

Covering wood floors only with area rugs was another way to diminish dust and dirt. The simple lines of Colonial Revival furniture fulfilled this desire for simplicity, cleanliness, and order.[3]

A writer for *House Beautiful* in 1904 testifies to the strength of the Colonial Revival movement:

Every year sees the Colonial reaching more perfect expression, not only in furniture but in hangings, draperies, and all the accesories of decoration. Even in the cheaper priced furniture exact Colonial reproductions may be had now, and the makers who are not content to depend on antiques alone for designs are producing a modern Colonial series that would have been creditable to Hepplewhite, Sheraton, or Chippendale. So we say that there will be no successor to the Colonial style. It is as near perfection in household furniture as can be created, and as such it needs no successor.[4]

A survey of furniture catalogues in the Winterthur Library from the early twentieth century confirms that Colonial Revival furniture was widely available. The designs vary greatly in historical accuracy, and the furniture itself varies in the quality of its construction. We should note, however, that furniture catalogues tend to reveal what was being made in fairly large shops rather than in the smaller shops, whose quality would be higher.

Given the popularity of Colonial styles, it is not surprising that quite a bit of the furniture available was not of the highest quality and was sold at low prices. Ekin Wallick's *Inexpensive Furnishing in Good Taste* (1915) includes a wide variety of factory-made, low-priced pieces in simplified forms, such as wing chairs, slant-front desks on straight legs, and stripped-down Sheraton-style dining-room pieces. The Sheraton style was recommended for its simple lines: "For a small apartment or country dining room there is probably no style of furniture more suitable than Sheraton. The simple gracefulness of its lines will add a certain dignity to any room. . . . Sheraton furniture calls for white woodwork and light colored walls and will lend itself admirably to any color scheme which might be chosen."[5] These inexpensive pieces were often made of gum, which was stained dark to look like mahogany. Some popular, relatively new forms in this book include pieces for men—smoking stands, book troughs, and book racks—and for women, new designs of sewing stands.

The 1910 catalogue of Brandt Cabinet Works of Hagerstown, Maryland, describes that company as makers of parlor and library tables. Brandt produced broad adaptations of Colonial designs, all of quartered oak or imitation mahogany. Most looked more like golden oak than anything from the eighteenth century.

In 1913, S. Karpen and Sons of Chicago, New York, and Boston advertised "Colonial suites," each consisting of a sofa, an easy chair, and a rocker. Most owe a debt to Empire design, with massive scrolling crest rails and arms and scrolling legs with upholstered backs and seats. These inexpensive suites were still heavily influenced by the massiveness of Victorian furniture, and most collectors today would not find them appealing.

Peck and Hills of New York, a large mail-order company, advertised Colonial Revival furniture in its 1916 catalogue, most of it in quartered oak, with some mahogany. There are dining-room suites in the Queen Anne and Sheraton styles,

---

3. Ibid., 116.

4. Quoted from Cheryl Robertson, "Women, Style, and Decoration: Inside the Colonial Revival Home," in *The Colonial Revival in Rhode Island*, 1890–1940 (Providence: Providence Preservation Society, 1989), 12.

5. Ekin Wallick, *Inexpensive Furnishings in Good Taste* (New York: Hearst's International Library Company, 1915), 91.

rather broadly interpreted, Jacobean furniture, and "period" tea carts—another popular item in the first quarter of the twentieth century.

The Danersk Furniture Company of New York advertised inexpensive-looking furniture in its 1917 catalogue, the most interesting being a gateleg desk consisting of a slant-front desk on a gateleg table base.

After 1900, and even more so after 1910, we see in furniture catalogues evidence of fairly faithful reproductions being manufactured in large numbers. By then, designers had absorbed some of the lessons offered by Irving Whitall Lyon in *The Colonial Furniture of New England,* which had been published in 1891, and Alvan Crocker Nye's 1895 book of designs of early American furniture, along with the period furniture included in the Hudson-Fulton Exhibition at the Metropolitan Museum. Well-researched books on American antiques continued to appear, such as Luke Vincent Lockwood's *Colonial Furniture in America* (1901). Lockwood's book covered the seventeenth century through the early nineteenth century, with furniture arranged according to period and style.

From 1900 on, many companies offered good-quality reproductions. Shaw's Furniture Company of Boston published a catalogue in 1910 with pen-and-ink drawings of elaborately carved Jacobean and Flemish pieces and living-room and dining-room suites in many styles. The quality appears high, though it is difficult to tell from the drawings alone.

The 1914 catalogue of the Richter Furniture Company of New York City shows many faithful adaptations of eighteenth-century designs, including Chippendale chairs of various grades. There is also a model called the "Puritan," a Queen Anne–style side chair with rockers, its selling price listed as $17.50.

Rocking chairs seem to have been irresistible to Colonial Revival designers.

A persuasive tribute to the popularity of Colonial Revival furniture during the 1910s is the 1915 *Craftsman* catalogue, which one would expect to find full of Mission furniture, identified with Gustav Stickley. Surprisingly, it also offered a number of Colonial designs, including several Chinese Chippendale pieces, Jacobean-inspired pieces with caning, a Windsor chair, a mahogany tilt-top table, a Chippendale pedestal, a gateleg table, and a mahogany slant-front desk.

Few of us associate Tiffany and Company with the Colonial Revival, but the company in fact did sell Colonial Revival furniture after 1907. Tiffany Studios had absorbed the Schmidt Brothers Furniture company in 1898. After 1907 Tiffany provided furnishings that it described as "artistic furniture" and "quality reproductions."[6] Tiffany catalogues from the 1910s show high-quality, generally faithful copies of dining-room and bedroom suites in many period styles (see figs. 4–1, 4–2, and 4–3).

Fig. 4-1 Duncan Phyfe-style mahogany extension table made by Tiffany Studios of New York City in 1915. Tiffany loosely described the table as being "in the Georgian style." Made from Cuban mahogany, it is inlaid with satinwood and ebony around the frieze. It sold for $215 in 1915. 5' diameter × 28¾" high (leaves each 14" × 60"). *Private collection.* **$2,400–3,600.**

6. Robert Koch, *Louis Tiffany: Rebel in Glass,* updated third edition (New York: Crown, 1982), 135, 136.

Fig. 4-2 Matching sideboard made by Tiffany Studios, 1915. With biscuit corners, serpentine front inlaid and crossbanded in satinwood and ebony. Legs are turned and reeded. Three cock-beaded drawers over one central drawer flanked by two cabinets. Shaped, beaded apron. Back with chamfered panels. Drawer interiors with quarter-molding. Shellac finish. Sold for $256 in 1915. 77″ long × 23½″ deep × 39″ high. *Private collection.* **$2,400–3,800.**

Fig. 4-3 Mahogany server to match sideboard and extension table, by Tiffany Studios, 1915. Three drawers above shelf. Sold for $113 in 1915. 46¼″ long × 20⅛″ deep × 35″ high. *Private collection.* **$900–1,200.**

Many small cabinet shops were making reproductions during this period. Nathan Margolis in Hartford, Connecticut, and Meier and Hagen in New York City are two of the better-known shops.

Nathan Margolis opened his cabinet-making shop in Hartford in 1893 after emigrating from Yanova, Russia. He began by restoring and selling antique furniture but soon concentrated on making reproductions. By the mid-1920s the Margolis Shop was doing a flourishing business in handmade reproductions. The shop records are now in the Winterthur Museum Library. Most of these records cover the years from 1925 to 1974, when Harold Margolis, Nathan's son, ran the business. The Margolis Shop made furniture for the upper-middle class, for whom Margolis furniture was a highly desirable alternative to the prohibitive cost of antiques. The majority of the craftsmen employed by Margolis were European immigrants, who brought with them a tradition of skilled woodworking (figs. 6–30 and 6–31).

In the manuscript collection at the Winterthur Library, we came across a billhead from 1911 from a New York City cabinetmaker, who advertised himself as "Caspar Sommerlad, Dr. Antique Furniture. Furniture made to order, repairing, upholstering and polishing. Furniture boxed and shipped." His billhead includes a drawing of a Colonial patriot holding a walking stick and wearing a tricorner hat and breeches standing next to a long-case clock, a mantel, and a Windsor chair.[7] No doubt there were many other small shops like Sommerlad's in every city.

At the turn of the century, Chicago had several makers of good-quality Colonial Revival furniture. Marshall Field & Company hired Frederick Walton who had been trained at the Art Institute of Chicago, to head its custom shop. In the 1910s Marshall Field made pieces according to the directions of decorators as well as its own in-house designs.[8]

Also in Chicago, W. K. Cowan and Company, founded in the 1890s, was showing Colonial Revival furniture in period rooms as early as 1906. By 1909 Cowan was making furniture in six hundred patterns and included Queen Anne, French Colonial, Chinese Chippendale, and Hepplewhite styles.[9]

The W. K. Cowan Company's 1915 catalogue, "Things Colonial," contains Empire Revival pieces masquerading as Colonial, in addition to a Washington writing table for $150 and a Martha Washington sewing table for $30 (for an example, see page 140). These two patriotic items became popular pieces. The Washington writing table was raised on reeded legs with a central drawer. The writing surface has shelves not on the back of the desk but on both sides and apparently was modeled after a desk used by Washington

in New York City (for a similar example, see page 142).

The David Zork Company in Chicago, founded in 1914, made and sold antiques and reproduction furniture, some of which was produced for midwestern interior designers.[10] A few years later, in 1920, the Chicago firm of Tapp, De Wilde and Wallace was established. It built a reputation for making top-quality, exact copies of existing pieces in eighteenth-century styles. It also produced designs gracefully adapted to modern living requirements, using the best woods and finished by hand. The furniture was sold in Chicago, New York, and Los Angeles.[11]

From the 1920s on, the Chicago company of Watson and Boaler imported European antiques and paneling. It also made its own reproductions, sometimes doctoring an actual antique, sometimes making the reproduction from scratch.[12]

Interest in the Colonial Revival reached a fever pitch in the 1920s with a series of important exhibits and the beginnings of the historic preservation movement, with the efforts of the Rockefellers in Williamsburg, Virginia, the du Pont family at Winterthur, near Wilmington, Delaware, and Henry Ford at Greenfield Village, in Dearborn, Michigan. In 1922 the Metropolitan Museum held an exhibition of Duncan Phyfe furniture. In the same year *The Magazine Antiques* was founded. The American Wing of The Metropolitan opened in 1924, featuring period rooms complete with paneling, furniture, and appropriate accessories on permanent display. The display was not limited to antiques from New England—now it also included the Midatlantic states and the South.

As Elizabeth Stillinger notes, exhibits

---

7. From the Joseph Downs Collection of Manuscripts and Ephemera, The Winterthur Library.

8. Sharon Darling, *Chicago Furniture: Art, Craft, and Industry, 1833–1983* (New York: W. W. Norton, 1984), 208.

9. Ibid., 210.

10. Ibid., 210, 211.

11. Ibid., 212.

12. Ibid.

47

in the American Wing, bringing together furniture with other decorative arts from the same style period for a complete experience, presented to the public a lesson in the aesthetics of the seventeenth and eighteenth centuries. Finally the public had learned to appreciate the more restrained and simple aesthetic of Colonial America without having to embellish it or "Victorianize" it. With the American Wing as one of the focal points of antiques in the country during the 1920s, New York overtook Boston as the country's leading antiques center. By 1930, *The Magazine Antiques* had moved from Boston to New York, as had the influential antiques dealer Israel Sack.[13]

Furniture manufacturers naturally made the most of the museum exhibits. In 1923, on the heels of the 1922 exhibit, Baker Furniture Company offered a line of Duncan Phyfe furniture. The Charlotte Furniture Company of Charlotte, Michigan, advertised itself as makers of "Reproductions and Adaptations of Antique Furniture." In a catalogue from the 1920s, many pieces are inspired by specific antiques from museums or important private collections. The catalogue included copies from the American Wing, the Bolles Collection in the Metropolitan Museum, the collections of Mrs. Frances Garvan and Wallace Nutting, and pieces featured in Lockwood's *Colonial Furniture in America.*

The 1920s continued to see mass-produced Colonial Revival furniture from Grand Rapids and the Midwest. One of the prospering midwestern manufacturers from the 1920s was Wilhelm Furniture of Sturgis, Michigan. Its 1924 catalogue showed spinet desks, gateleg tables, tea carts, and other popular items. One intriguing catalogue from around the 1920s is from the Hand Made Furniture Shop of Chicago, advertising a "complete line of correct tea carts and ferneries." This com-

pany, and many others, produced tea carts in all the popular styles—Chippendale, Queen Anne, William and Mary, Adam, Jacobean, Sheraton, and "Colonial." In mahogany, a tea cart was priced around $40; in oak, $35.

Paine Furniture Company of Boston continued to produce large quantities of Colonial Revival furniture. Its catalogues from about 1920 show "Colonial style" (read "Empire style") twin beds, wing chairs, "Colonial sideboards" (which look like Empire pieces), music stands and "tip tables."

The 1920s witnessed the application of Colonial styles to new forms, such as coffee tables, tea carts, telephone tables, book stands, and radio tables. One mail-order company offering these new forms was the W. A. Hathaway Company of New York City. Its 1924 catalogue, "Furniture for the Home Emphasizing the Early American Period," showed desks of many forms (spinet, kneehole, George Washington), sofas, chairs, telephone cabinets, tea carts, and more. Judging from the catalogue, "Colonial" referred to Empire style, and "Early American" pieces were spool-turned.

The catalogue for the Winthrop Furniture Company in Boston from about 1925 shows another adaptation of the popular gateleg form. Winthrop offered a "Colonial Gateleg Corner Cabinet"—an odd-looking piece of furniture, consisting of a cabinet with a broken-arch pediment and central flame finial above doors with gothic arches. Below is the gateleg table with an oval top. In the same catalogue, Winthrop offered a mahogany library table with quarter-columns, cabriole legs, and ball-and-claw feet—sort of an elongated lowboy form, and one that is popular with buyers today (see a similar example on page 126). The catalogue also shows a "Colonial Chest," said to be an exact reproduction of a Salem (Massachu-

---

13. Stillinger, *The Antiquers,* 196–97.

48

setts) chest, a tallish chest with fluted quarter-columns and fan-carved apron (see page 143 for a similar chest).

Leavens of Boston, which sold mass-produced furniture in the 1920s, took liberties with earlier styles, applying older design motifs to new forms, such as telephone sets, gateleg desks, and smoking stands.

Although many companies in the 1920s made low-priced mass-produced Colonial Revival furniture, some companies sought to distinguish themselves from the fray and made good-quality, well-designed reproductions. A catalogue from about 1920 for the Old Colony Furniture Company of Boston and New York emphasizes the high quality of its furniture. With a design department headed by an antiquarian of note, Old Colony produced furniture that, according to the catalogue, was all handmade and hand-carved, with no spindle carving. Furthermore, the finishes were hand-rubbed. The company made bedroom suites, cabinets, chairs, desks, secretaries, mirrors, sideboards, sofas, and tables, as well as other furniture.

In the 1920s, the Kensington Manufacturing Company of New York City made good pieces in the Hepplewhite, Duncan Phyfe, Sheraton, seventeenth-century English, and Italian Renaissance styles. Kensington won a gold medal for craftsmanship at the 39th Annual Exhibition of the Architectural League in 1924. The award was for excellence in design, restraint in the treatment of details, workmanship (joinery, carving), and versatility of styles and periods.

The Chicago companies that were making reproductions included Watson and Boaler, John A. Colby & Sons, and Tapp, De Wilde and Wallace. Cleveland was the home of the design firm Rorimer-Brooks, known for its fine custom furniture. In the 1920s and 1930s, to meet public demand, Rorimer-Brooks also made Colonial Revival pieces in William and Mary, Queen Anne, and Duncan Phyfe styles. Some were faithful reproductions, and some were made using old parts.[14]

Ferdinand Keller of Philadelphia advertised in "Antiques, Reproductions," a catalogue of about 1920, good-quality pieces that were largely handmade, in the styles of Duncan Phyfe, Hepplewhite, Queen Anne, and Elizabethan. Karcher and Rehm was also making Colonial Revival furniture in Philadelphia around the same time.

The 1920s also saw the rise to prominence of such large department stores as Wanamaker's, Lord & Taylor, Jordan Marsh, and Marshall Field, some of which sent their buyers to Europe in search of antiques. Wanamaker's, of New York and Philadelphia, sold excellent-quality reproductions from many different periods in suites and as individual pieces. Beginning in 1918, Wanamaker's offered the first department-store decorating service, called "Au Quatrieme," in the New York store.[15]

Wanamaker's had offered Colonial Revival pieces as early as 1887 in its mail-order catalogue, where it advertised a library chair with a mahogany frame in the "English wing pattern" for $42.50 and a three-piece parlor suite (a settee, armchair, and side chair), featuring solid mahogany frames, in a generally faithful Sheraton square-back style. Also advertised were bedroom, dining-room, and desk chairs in a Chippendale style of rather elongated proportions.

By the 1920s Wanamaker's was advertising its high-quality Colonial-style furniture with finesse. Its 1927 catalogue, "Reflections in Good Taste," featured

14. Leslie Pina, *Louis Rorimer: A Man of Style* (Kent, Ohio: Kent State University Press, 1990), 48–49.
15. Ibid., 38.

room settings with an elegant, though lived-in, look. In each photograph, something is nonchalantly draped over a chair—a bathrobe, a towel, etc. Each photograph is described in breezy terms, casually invoking historical figures. The illustration of a study is entitled "Things to think with" and includes a George Washington desk and a John Hancock chair. Another library scene is labeled "In the Jeffersonian key." "Chippendale, Moderato" describes a comfortable living room, complete with camelback sofa, kneehole desk, lowboy, and tennis racket.

Fine department stores on the West Coast, notably S. and G. Gump Company of San Francisco, sold Colonial Revival furniture and other styles. Gump's catalogue, "Furniture of Individuality," included furniture copying Jacobean, early Italian, Renaissance, Louis XV, and Louis XVI styles.

In the 1920s Wallace Nutting in Massachusetts and Nathan Margolis and Abraham Fineberg in Hartford, Connecticut, were producing good-quality furniture. High-quality bench-made reproductions were being made in New England towns and elsewhere. In most areas where there was any money at all, by the 1920s and certainly by the 1930s, local cabinetmakers in small shops were selling their furniture locally to people of means. Figure 4–4 shows an example of a fine-quality bench-made reproduction made around 1930 in a shop in North Carolina.

The 1920s were famous for conspicuous consumption, and this was demonstrated in the antiques world as well. The decade ended with two highly publicized auctions of American antiques—the Reifsnyder Sale and the Flayderman Sale, both held in New York City in 1929. These two sales brought staggering prices

Fig. 4-4 Handmade copy of an eighteenth-century lowboy, c. 1930, made in a small cabinetmaking shop in Elizabeth City, North Carolina. A copy of a local c. 1760 piece. Cabriole legs with volutes, pad feet. Shell-carved apron. Walnut. 34⅛″ wide × 24⅜″ deep × 28¾″ high. *Private collection.* **$1,800–2,600.**

as a result of the competition between the major collectors Henry Ford, Henry Frances du Pont, and Frances Garvan. These millionaire collectors certainly impressed upon the public the value and importance of American antiques.[16]

The 1920s ended with the Girl Scouts Loan Exhibition in New York City in 1929, an important exhibit that widened its focus on American antiques from seventeenth-century New England to include New York and Pennsylvania and Queen Anne, Chippendale, and Duncan Phyfe styles. This exhibition brought together the cream of the crop of American antiques, each piece having been carefully selected to demonstrate the best design characteristics of its kind. By the end of the 1920s American antiques were without question validated for their artistic merit.[17] As the public demanded copies of the finest museum-quality American antiques, the market for reproductions became increasingly strong.

---

16. Stillinger, *The Antiquers,* 200–202.

17. Ibid., 202–3

5

The Furniture of Wallace Nutting

By Michael Ivankovich

Michael Ivankovich is widely recognized as the country's leading authority on Wallace Nutting pictures, books, and furniture. He is the author of four books on Wallace Nutting, including The Guide to Wallace Nutting Furniture, The Price Guide to Wallace Nutting Pictures *(4th edition),* The Alphabetical and Numerical Index to Wallace Nutting Pictures, *and* The Guide to Wallace Nutting–Like Photographers of the Early Twentieth Century. *He has also published five other reference guides on Wallace Nutting and has written numerous articles. He conducts periodic Wallace Nutting specialty auctions. Ivankovich can be reached at P.O. Box 2458, Doylestown, PA 18901; (215) 345-6094.*

Many people no doubt know the name Wallace Nutting from his landscape photographs, and some may be aware that he wrote nearly twenty books, but, surprisingly, relatively few people know much about Wallace Nutting's bench-made reproduction furniture.

Working in Southbury, Connecticut, from 1905 to 1912, Wallace Nutting, a retired Congregational minister, moved his already profitable picture business to Framingham, Massachusetts, where it began to flourish. He sold his pictures in department stores and gift shops, and the public soon became fascinated by his pleasant pastoral scenes of flowering trees, birches, streams, and lakes. By 1912 Nutting's picture business was grossing more than a thousand dollars a day.

As the public became more interested in the Colonial Revival movement, Nutting began to compose and photograph Colonial interior scenes in his home or in the homes of friends. He would dress his models in Colonial outfits and pose them among fine antiques and decorative items of various forms and styles.

Over a five-year period, starting in 1915, Nutting purchased, restored, and furnished five historic homes in New England. Each house was selected because of its historical charm and its particular decorative style. These houses were the Wentworth-Gardner House in Portsmouth, New Hampshire (Chippendale style); the Hazen-Garrison House in Haverhill, Massachusetts (Pilgrim, with English influence); the Culter-Bartlett House in Newburyport, Massachusetts (Chippendale, Hepplewhite, and Sheraton); the Saugus Iron Works, or Broadhearth, in Saugus, Massachusetts (Pilgrim with Gothic influence); and the Webb House in Wethersfield, Connecticut (Dutch and Chippendale).

As a result of his research into such a wide variety of styles during these five years, Nutting became recognized as an expert of early American antiques. The lack of scholarship on early American antiques led Nutting to write and publish three books of his own. His first book, *Windsor Chairs* (see figure 5–1), published in 1917, became the definitive work on Windsor chairs. In 1921 Nutting published a book on Pilgrim-style furniture, *Furniture of the Pilgrim Century* (see figure 5–2), and in 1928 he published *The Furniture Treasury,* which is still in print and is still considered to be the most complete pictorial reference book on early American antiques.

Nutting knew that he was only one of many collectors of antiques. As early as 1915, with the Colonial Revival movement well under way, the finest examples of early American antiques were frequently unavailable even to those who

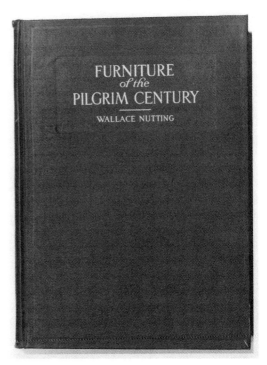

Fig. 5-2 Wallace Nutting's *Furniture of the Pilgrim Century,* published in 1921, covered not only Windsors but also other types of chairs, American chests, desks, tables, mirrors, clocks, utensils, and hardware. More than five hundred pages long, with more than a thousand photographs of items dating from 1620 to 1720. This was the period from which the early Nutting reproductions were taken. *Courtesy Michael Ivankovich, Diamond Press.*

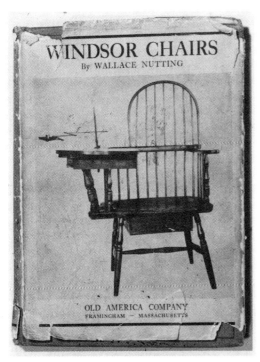

Fig. 5-1 Wallace Nutting's 1917 book on American Windsors, the first serious study of the Windsor form, discusses chairs from 1725 to 1825 and pictures nearly one hundred Windsors, many of which Nutting owned himself. *Courtesy Michael Ivankovich, Diamond Press.*

could afford them. Thus Nutting decided, in 1917, to start his own furniture reproduction business.

In 1918 Nutting published his first reproduction furniture catalogue, this one on Windsor Chairs (see figure 5–3). Nutting had become an expert on Windsor chairs, so, logically, this was the first style he began reproducing. His sales catalogue contained more than one hundred different Windsor styles that were available from his shop. Nutting continued producing Windsor chairs through the 1930s, so Windsors account for a large percentage of his production and are the most common, available form of Wallace Nutting furniture. When Nutting decided to create the "perfect" Windsor chair, he could use as a

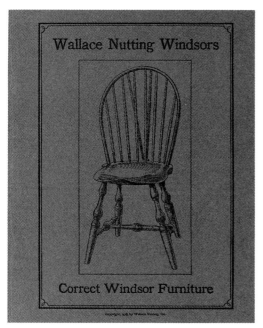

Fig. 5-3 Wallace Nutting's 1918 catalogue of Windsor chairs from his workshop, his first furniture sales catalogue. *Courtesy Michael Ivankovich, Diamond Press.*

Fig. 5-4 Wallace Nutting c. 1921 no. 420 bow-back Windsor armchair with a block brand. Fairly common. Very good condition. 41″ high. *Courtesy Michael Ivankovich, Diamond Press,* **$1,000–1,500.**

model one of the 150 Windsors in his own collection.

Nutting made his Windsors entirely by hand, even though he could have made them by machine for one-twentieth of the cost of hand production. With so much handwork involved, a craftsman was capable of completing only three or four chair seats a day. Each seat was shaped from a single piece of country pine 2″ thick. All legs and stretchers were finished on a hand lathe because machine lathes could not make cuts deep enough for the look Nutting wanted to achieve. All chair legs were raked 4″ within 18″ in order to provide the greatest strength and stability. Bow backs and combs were bent with wet steam and shaped by hand. Arm rails ending in knuckles were carved by hand.

Nutting used three different woods in making his Windsors: rock maple for the legs, country pine for the seats, and hickory for the spindles, bows, bent arm rails, and combs. The finishing process was an important part of Windsor construction. Each part of the chair was finished at least five times by hand with a special shellac. The chairs were rubbed by hand between each coat.

After mastering the Windsor form, Nutting designed furniture in the Pilgrim Century style. He made court cupboards, paneled and sunflower chests, oak chests, tables of many designs, including butterfly, gateleg, refectory, trestle, folding gate, and tavern tables, framed desks, ladderback chairs, joined and rush stools, and pilgrim and Carver chairs. He ventured into other styles only when forced to do so by economic pressures. As he wrote in the *Wallace Nutting General Catalogue, Supreme Edition* in 1930, "a stop is made just short of the cabriole leg." In the mid-1920s Nutting began to sell other furniture styles in order to maintain his business's profitability: Chippendale, Hepplewhite, Queen Anne, Sheraton, Duncan Phyfe,

Fig. 5-5 Wallace Nutting c. 1921 no. 329 swivel Windsor side chair with a block brand. Unusual, but not rare. Normal wear. 18″ wide × 16¾″ deep × 40″ high. *Courtesy Michael Ivankovich, Diamond Press,* **$400–650.**

Fig. 5-6 Wallace Nutting c. 1921 no. 415 comb-back Windsor chair with New England turnings and block brand. Unusual, but not rare. Very good condition. 45″ tall. *Private collection.* **$1,000–1,500.**

Federal—he copied them all. His advertisements in *The Magazine Antiques* helped him reach an affluent market.

At his peak, Nutting employed about twenty-five craftsmen. By 1927–28, however, sales had begun to lag. Nutting was aware of the demand for eighteenth-century designs, so he began to copy Queen Anne, Chippendale, Hepplewhite, and Sheraton styles. In his autobiography he wrote: "My first attempt at mahogany was to copy the most beautiful and elaborate piece of American furniture—a secretary in Providence which had been bought from Goddard. I took six of my craftsmen to study it by the hour and to make all measurements and sketches. . . . I knew if I had made that piece as well as the old,

that I could make anything." In the late 1920s he produced Savery (of Philadelphia) style highboys and lowboys, Queen Anne, Chippendale, and Hepplewhite style armchairs and side chairs, carved walnut sideboards, a Goddard chest-on-chest, Welsh dressers, and a carved corner cupboard. In all, Nutting offered eighty different types of chairs, thirty beds, sixty tables, twenty chests and chests of drawers, twenty cupboards, and twenty desks and secretaries.

Nutting took an analytical approach to the furniture reproduction process. First, he would locate the finest examples of authentic American antiques. After studying each piece with his master craftsmen, they would draw detailed

Fig. 5-7 Pair of Wallace Nutting c. 1921 no. 333 Windsor comb-back side chairs, block branded. Unusual, but not rare. Normal wear. 44″ tall. **$1,500–2,000** the pair. *Center:* Wallace Nutting c. 1921 no. 660 tavern table, block brand. Unusual, but not rare. Normal wear. 36″ wide × 24″ deep × 27″ high. **$1,000–1,500.** Pair of Wallace Nutting c. 1921 no. 22 cross-base candlestands, one with block brand, one unmarked. Unusual, but not rare. Normal wear. 14″ diameter × 25″ high. *Courtesy Northeast Auctions, Hampton, New Hampshire.* **$300–500** each.

sketches to determine what made each piece unique.

Rarely did he find an antique he felt was perfect. To him, most pieces needed some improvement—and extra inch added to the legs, a crisper turning, a narrower drawer. He then incorporated these improvements in his final drawings and sketches.

After deciding which pieces to reproduce, Nutting drew precise patterns. His craftsmen used the patterns, whether of paper or wood, to ensure uniformity in size for each individual component. The final step before production was to assemble a model of the piece of furniture. Every craftsman was required to duplicate the master prototype exactly. Once a piece reached the production stage, Nutting as-

signed it a three-digit Furniture Design Number for his sales catalogues. For example, the 300s represented side chairs, the 400s were armchairs, the 900s were cabinet pieces, etc.

Nutting's furniture reproductions represented one of the finest styles of any twentieth-century furniture maker. What sets his furniture apart was his production method. He insisted that his craftsmen follow the old, traditional methods. All turnings and carvings were executed by hand, and all assembly was done with foxtail wedges and hot glue. Each step contributed to a finer, more accurate piece of furniture. Nutting, however, never cut corners and produced each piece regardless of expense.

Maintaining such a high level of qual-

Fig. 5-8 Pair of Wallace Nutting c. 1921 no. 408 bow-back Windsor armchairs with block brands. Unusual, but not rare. Normal wear. 41″ tall. *Courtesy Northeast Auctions, Hampton, New Hampshire.* **$2,000–3,000** the pair.

ity had its consequences. Nutting's furniture was expensive, and the Depression signaled the decline of his business. Nutting had always relied on his picture business to carry the furniture business. Now the picture business was hard hit as well. By 1930 Nutting was making a commercial line of furniture for businesses—check-writing desks for banks, typewriter desks, executive desks, stenographer's chairs, a spinning-wheel hatrack, and even an oak radiator cover. By the late 1930s, he had only three or four employees.

Wallace Nutting died in 1941, and his remaining furniture and antique collection was sold at Parke-Bernet in New York.

Markings

Wallace Nutting marked most of his furniture using one of five distinct markings:

1. Paper labels were Nutting's earliest form of identification; he used three different labels between 1917 and 1922.

2. Script-branded signature: In 1922, Nutting sold his business, along with the right to continue using the Wallace Nutting name. The new owners did not maintain Nutting's high standards, and in 1924 Nutting repurchased the business. Although script-branded furniture is collect-

Fig. 5-9 Set of eight Wallace Nutting c. 1921 no. 408 bow-back Windsor armchairs, block branded. A set of eight is rare; this is an assembled set. Normal wear. 41″ high. *Courtesy Northeast Auctions, Hampton, New Hampshire.* **$8,000–12,000.**

ible in its own right, it is not as desirable as paper-label and block-branded furniture.

3. Block-branded signature: From 1924 to his death in 1941, Nutting marked his furniture with a distinctive block brand. This marking indicates furniture that was made *after* Nutting repurchased his business.

4. Punched, or incised, marking: This much smaller, block-type marking was usually used on small items such as treenware. This marking can be found on significantly larger pieces as well, such as chairs, tables, and corner cupboards.

5. Punched number: Some pieces of Nutting furniture retain their three-digit punched number, although the paper label may be missing.

Wallace Nutting Fakes

At present, fake Wallace Nutting furniture presents minimal problems. Pieces of inferior furniture marked with a fake, stenciled "Wallace Nutting" are rare.

Fig. 5-10 Set of six Wallace Nutting c. 1921 no. 301 bow-back, brace-back side chairs, block branded. Individual chairs are fairly common; sets are unusual, but not rare. Normal wear, 39″ tall. *Courtesy Northeast Auctions, Hampton, New Hampshire.* **$3,000–5,000.**

The best defense against fake Wallace Nutting furniture is to learn the difference between ordinary and superior examples. Nutting represents the finest of twentieth-century reproductions available, and, although anyone can fake a paper label or a branded signature, no one can profitably reproduce a piece of fine Nutting furniture, add seventy-five years of age and patina, and make it look as good as the original.

The Future of Wallace Nutting Furniture

Wallace Nutting furniture can be found in shops and shows all over the country, but especially in New England, where it was originally made. Over the past several years, major regional auction houses have included significant amounts of Nutting furniture. In 1989 Skinner's of Bolton, Massachusetts, had a sale devoted entirely to Nutting and a few other makers of fine reproductions.

A highly successful March 1992 auction at Northeast Auctions in New Hamp-

Fig. 5-11 Set of six Wallace Nutting c. 1921 no. 393 Pilgrim side chairs, block branded. Individual chairs are fairly common; sets are unusual, but not rare. Normal wear, except for damaged rush on several seats. 43″ tall. *Courtesy Northeast Auctions, Hampton New Hampshire.* **$800–1,600** for the set, as is. If rush in good condition, **$1,500–2,400.**

shire contained over twenty lots of Wallace Nutting furniture. Several lots consisted of sets of chairs and commanded substantial prices.

A January 1993 Americana sale at Sotheby's in New York City contained four lots of exceptional Wallace Nutting furniture, three of which sold for well over estimate. A Chippendale-style shell-carved secretary in the Newport manner sold for almost $15,000; a Federal-style desk with bookcase sold for $3450; a Chippendale-style bonnet-top highboy with shell carving sold for over $7000; and a Chippendale-style lowboy sold for $3162. All of these were formal pieces, made in styles that Nutting turned to in the late 1920s, after his Pilgrim Century pieces. His high style pieces will probably continue to command the highest prices. With such major auction houses selling Nutting furniture, we can assume that the market for Wallace Nutting furniture is in a strong position to improve into the twenty-first century.

Fig. 5-12 Set of eight Wallace Nutting c. 1921 New England ladder-back chairs (two no. 490 armchairs, six no. 390 side chairs), block branded. Individual chairs are fairly common; sets are unusual, but not rare. Normal wear, except for damaged rush on several seats. 50″ tall. *Courtesy Northeast Auctions, Hampton, New Hampshire.* **$1,800–3,000** the set, as is. In good condition, the set would sell for **$2,500–4,500.**

Fig. 5-13 Two armchairs from a set of eight Wallace Nutting c. 1928 ribbon-back Chippendale chairs (*two* no. 459-B armchairs, *six* no. 359-B side chairs), block branded. Individual chairs are rare; sets are extremely rare. Normal wear. 40″ tall. *Courtesy C. G. Sloan and Company. North Bethesda, Maryland.* **$4,000–6,000.**

Fig. 5-14 Set of four Wallace Nutting c. 1928 Queen Anne–style mahogany side chairs (similar to no 399), branded signature. Extremely rare. 42½″ high. *Courtesy Skinner, Inc., Bolton, Mass.* Single, **$750–1,000.** Four for **$3,000–4,000.** Eight for **$6,000–8,000.**

Fig 5-15 Wallace Nutting c. 1928 upholstered wing chair with large ball-and-claw feet, carved legs, and block and turned stretcher base. *Courtesy Nadeau's Auction Gallery, Windsor, Conn.* **$2,500–3,500.**

Fig. 5-17 Wallace Nutting c. 1921 no. 17 Windsor candlestand, block brand. Fairly common. Excellent condition. 14″ diameter × 25″ high. *Courtesy Michael Ivankovich, Diamond Press.* **$350–500.**

Fig. 5-16 Wallace Nutting c. 1928 no. 525 Chippendale-style mahogany sofa, no visible signature. Extremely rare. 75″ long × 37″ high. *Courtesy Skinner, Inc., Bolton, Mass.* **$1,500–2,200.**

Fig. 5-19 Wallace Nutting c. 1928 large Chippendale-style giltwood and mahogany-veneer looking glass, branded signature. Rare. 53″ high. *Courtesy Skinner, Inc., Bolton, Mass.* **$1,000–1,500.**

Fig. 5-18 Wallace Nutting c. 1920s no. 903 spoon rack, unmarked. Extremely rare. Normal wear (this piece is in its original red paint, which is quite unusual). 24¾″ high. *Courtesy Michael Ivankovich, Diamond Press.* **$350–500.**

Fig. 5-20 Wallace Nutting c. 1928 no. 693B Chippendale-style carved mahogany piecrust tip-top tea table, branded signature. Rare. 27½″ high × 33″ diameter. *Courtesy Skinner, Inc., Bolton, Mass.* **$1,800–2,400.**

Fig. 5-21 Wallace Nutting c. 1921 no. 615 trestle table, block brand. Unusual, but not rare. Very good condition. 50″ long × 30″ high. *Courtesy Michael Ivankovich, Diamond Press.* **$600–900.**

Fig. 5-22 Wallace Nutting c. 1921 no. 613 ball-turned tavern table with paper label. Rare. Very good condition. 36″ × 25½″. *Courtesy Michael Ivankovich, Diamond Press.* **$800–1,200.**

Fig. 5-23 Wallace Nutting c. 1928 block-front chest with four graduated drawers, bracket feet. Top is molded and shaped. Drawer openings are lipped. Rare. A 1940 advertisement in *The Magazine Antiques* described it as "one of the simplest examples of the Goddard style. Heavy Cuban mahogany in three-inch thickness used for the drawers." *Courtesy James D. Julia, Inc., Fairfield, Maine.* **$1,500–2,400.**

Fig. 5-24 Wallace Nutting c. 1928 no. 979 Chippendale-style mahogany bureau in the Goddard manner, branded signature. Extremely rare. 39½″ wide × 18½″ deep × 34¾″ high. *Courtesy Skinner, Inc., Bolton, Mass.* **$3,000–5,000.**

Fig. 5-25 Wallace Nutting c. 1928 no. 729 Chippendale-style maple slant-front desk, branded signature. Rare. 36″ wide × 19″ deep × 39″ high. *Courtesy Skinner, Inc., Bolton, Mass.* **$1,800–2,400.**

Fig. 5-26 Wallace Nutting c. 1928 no. 729 Chippendale-style mahogany blind-door secretary, branded signature. Extremely rare. 42″ wide × 23″ deep × 103″ high. *Courtesy Skinner, Inc., Bolton, Mass.* **$8,000–12,000.**

Fig. 5-27 Wallace Nutting c. 1928 no. 989 Chippendale-style mahogany highboy, unsigned. Extremely rare. 39½″ wide × 20″ deep × 85½″ high. *Courtesy Skinner, Inc., Bolton, Mass.* **$4,000–7,500.**

Fig. 5-29 Wallace Nutting c. 1928 no. 846B Federal-style maple tester bed, branded signature, with net and dust ruffle. Rare. 54″ wide × 76½″ long × 68″ high. *Courtesy Skinner, Inc., Bolton, Mass.* **$1,200–1,800.**

Fig. 5-28 Wallace Nutting c. 1928 no. 832B Federal-style carved mahogany tester bed, branded signature, with net and dust ruffle. Rare. 54″ wide × 74″ long × 82″ high. *Courtesy Skinner, Inc., Bolton, Mass.* **$1,200–1,800.**

6

The 1930s: Diverted by the Depression

The Depression brought an abrupt end to the public's eager acquisition of all things Colonial. The interest may have continued to exist, but the means to buy did not. The decline of Wallace Nutting's furniture business can be taken as an example of the toll exacted by the Depression. Colonial styles remained popular, but the general public simply could not afford to buy as it had in the 1920s. Not surprisingly, many furniture companies failed completely.

By the end of the Depression, several changes were evident in the furniture industry as a whole. The South, with its cheap labor and plentiful raw materials, had emerged as a powerful new furniture producer, overtaking Grand Rapids as a maker of low-grade residential furniture. Furniture manufacturers in the Midwest, New York, and other areas responded to the Depression by marketing smaller pieces, when the public could not afford to buy large case pieces. Popular items included magazine racks, radio cabinets, and telephone stands—all made in a variety of period styles. The production of these novelty items helped places like Chicago and New York maintain their furniture production throughout the 1930s.

Finally, several companies capitalized on the partnership between museums and the Colonial Revival movement that had begun in the 1920s. These companies were granted the rights to reproduce items from museum collections. This trend has lasted through the decades and, in recent years, several museums have strengthened their furniture reproduction programs, providing the public with a good source of reproductions.

During the 1930s Grand Rapids was losing its grip on the market for low-end furniture. Grand Rapids continued to produce high-quality expensive furniture, but it was not able to compete with the low-priced furniture being produced in the South in increasing quantities in the 1920s and 30s.

The Southern furniture industry had been in existence from the 1880s, soon after the Civil War and Reconstruction, making inexpensive furniture for Southerners recovering from the economic deprivations of war. Furniture factories in North Carolina, Georgia, Virginia, and Tennessee were locally owned, and produced furniture largely for the local population. It was not marketed widely. However, the South had abundant lumber and cheap labor: fine potential for a successful furniture industry.

During the last quarter of the nineteenth century, as many of the large furniture manufacturers moved from the Northeast to the Midwest, some of the Northeastern firms began to explore opportunities in the South, and began to in-

Fig. 6-1 The display room of the Continental Furniture Company of High Point, North Carolina, in 1936. Continental prospered throughout the 1920s and 1930s. Displayed are Chippendale-style secretary-bookcases, kneehole desks, a block-front slant-lid desk, Windsor chairs, and ladder-back chairs. *Courtesy Kate Cloninger, International Home Furnishings Center, High Point, N.C.*

vest in already existing factories there. By 1890 North Carolina had six furniture factories; by 1900 this number had increased to forty-four, with twelve of those plants located in High Point, indicating an early strength that would solidify in the twentieth century.[1]

High Point copied the same proven marketing strategies used in Grand Rapids. Furniture manufacturers came together in High Point to pool their strengths and compete more effectively against Grand Rapids, rather than compete against one another. In 1913 High Point had its first semiannual Southern Furniture Exposition, patterned after the Furniture Market in Grand Rapids. The first Exposition consisted mainly of cheap and medium-grade bedroom furniture, including pieces in Colonial styles. Not only

did furniture manufacturers participate in the Exposition, but suppliers of materials attended as well. Lewis Thompson and Company, a Philadelphia firm then the largest handler of mahogany in the world, owning 640,000 acres of timberland in Mexico, was on hand to display its mahogany and Circassian walnut veneers.[2]

World War I disrupted the progress of the Southern Furniture Exposition, but only temporarily. By the mid-1920s, High Point's exposition was attracting national attention and it led to the growth of the furniture industry not only in North Carolina, but also in Tennessee, Georgia, and Virginia (figures 6–1 and 6–2 illustrate the work of two High Point area companies). By 1926 North Carolina had 133 factories, while Tennessee, Georgia, and Virginia combined had 100 factories. During

1. David N. Thomas, "A History of Southern Furniture," *Furniture South* 46, no. 10, sec. 2 (October 1967): 14, 25.
2. Ibid., 37, 46, 47.

Fig. 6-2 Chippendale-style c. 1930 mahogany kneehole desk with shell-carved apron, fluted quarter-columns, cabriole legs, pad feet. Labeled "Thomasville Chair Co. Character Furniture Since 1904." From the High Point, North Carolina area. 49″ long × 19½″ deep × 30″ high. *Courtesy Willow Park Mall, Durham, N.C.* **$900–1,200.**

the 1920s, the North Carolina furniture industry produced more bedroom and dining room furniture than any other part of the country. By 1929 producers from most of the important furniture-making centers attended the semiannual Exposition.[3]

The Depression slowed the progress of the Southern furniture industry for a few years, but as the nation began to recover from the Depression, it was clear that High Point had surpassed Grand Rapids in the production of cheap and medium-range furniture for the general public. By 1937 North Carolina and Virginia were producing 38 percent of the country's bedroom furniture and 37 percent of its dining room furniture. In 1937 North Carolina ranked second after New York in overall furniture production.[4]

Most of the Southern companies began the same way the Grand Rapids companies began: dealing with the raw product, making wood products, and then making furniture using mass production. There were, however, smaller cabinet shops also producing higher-quality furniture. One such firm that grew into a successful company throughout the first half of the twentieth century was Biggs Furniture Company of Richmond, Virginia. Biggs is an example of the firms producing high-quality bench-made reproductions in the 1930s.

Like many businesses specializing in reproductions, Biggs began with a cabinetmaker who knew antiques, who repaired them, and soon got into the profitable business of making reproductions. In 1890 Joseph Franklin Biggs, an En-

---

3. Ibid., p. 55, 59, 66.

4. Ibid., p. 72.

glishman, opened up his shop in Richmond. Apparently, he came to Virginia looking for antiques to sell. When he realized that his customers would sometimes be forced to wait a year before he could locate the antiques they wanted, he began to make reproductions. Biggs copied originals for his customers and he gradually built up the business to employ many craftsmen to produce handmade reproductions. Biggs also continued to carry antiques until the 1930s. Eventually, Biggs had shops in Atlanta, Washington, Baltimore, Pittsburgh, and New Orleans. In the 1930s Biggs had a flourishing mail-order business, with catalogues advertising "Fine Colonial Reproductions" (see figure 6–3). Biggs pieces were popular throughout the South, and Biggs reproductions show up for sale all around the country today. Though acquired by several larger firms, Biggs continued to do business in Richmond until 1989.

Also in Richmond, and for a while next door to Biggs, was H. C. Valentine

Fig. 6-3 Biggs Furniture Company catalogue from the early 1940s, Richmond, Virginia.

and Company, which produced bench-made furniture of the same quality, using similar designs (see figures 6–4 and 6–5). Valentine's catalogue from around 1930 contains a series of individual pamphlets on each American style period, even "Colonial," which they admit to be Empire style (they continue to use the term "Colonial" because the public seemed to insist on it). Each pamphlet provides a brief history of the style, and illustrates several pieces made by Valentine in that particular style. Valentine apparently started out as an antiques dealer and appraiser who employed craftsmen to build reproductions. Valentine's catalogue claims that no modern methods were used in the shop. Finishes were hand-applied and hand-rubbed, with at least seven coats of finish. During the 1930s Valentine sold antiques as well as reproductions. Although Biggs continued to expand its business throughout the 1930s, Valentine must have suffered during the Depression, as the business did not survive the 1930s.

One large Virginia firm that prospered during the first half of the twentieth century was Bassett Furniture Industries. Bassett was founded in 1902, by J. D. Bassett, who began by selling oak lumber to companies in Grand Rapids and Jamestown, New York. Then Bassett began to produce bedroom suites in golden oak. Prices were cheap—one bed actually sold for $1.50. As the firm prospered and hired furniture designers, it began to produce some Colonial designs, like those shown in figure 6–6. During the 1930s, eighteenth-century styles in mahogany were popular sellers.

Southern furniture companies also forged relationships with regional museums to make reproductions from their collections. Virginia Craftsmen, Inc. of Harrisonburg was granted exclusive rights to reproduce antiques from Monticello, home of Thomas Jefferson. Pieces shown in the catalogue included Jefferson's music rack, a card table, and a sewing table.

Fig. 6-4 The showrooms of H. C. Valentine Company, Richmond, Virginia, showing its period reproductions. From the H. C. Valentine Company catalogue, c. 1930.

Fig. 6-5 The showrooms from the H. C. Valentine Company, Richmond, Virginia, showing a variety of Chippendale, Empire, and other period reproductions for the dining room. From the H. C. Valentine Company catalogue, c. 1930.

Fig. 6-6 Bassett Furniture Industries Jacobean-style dining-room suite from the 1920s. Mahogany and walnut. Gate-leg table with molded top and Jacobean-type turnings. Chairs with cutout carrying handles, strong turnings. Buffet and server complete the set. *Courtesy Bassett Furniture Industries, Bassett, Virginia.*

In the late 1940s, Biggs took over the furniture reproduction program at Monticello.

Other museums around the country also began sponsoring reproductions in the 1930s. In 1936, Kittinger began reproducing selected pieces for Colonial Williamsburg. This relationship continued until 1989, when Kittinger went out of business. Baker Furniture Company makes the Colonial Williamsburg reproductions today. In Zeeland, Michigan, the Colonial Manufacturing Company began making reproductions for the Henry Ford Museum in Dearborn, including several tall case clocks (Colonial's specialty), corner chairs, a tambour desk, highboys, and several Duncan Phyfe-style pieces. Colonial continued making reproductions for the Henry Ford Museum into the 1960s.

Individual craftsmen working in small cabinetmaking shops also continued to make high-quality, largely handmade reproductions, often based on a local antique. In Baltimore, Potthast Brothers continued making high-quality reproductions, as did J. W. Berry and Son. Enrico Liberti opened up his Baltimore shop in the 1930s. The Liberti Shop built an excellent reputation during the 1930s and was employed to make reproductions for a number of public buildings. Liberti still makes reproductions today.

In Hartford, Connecticut, the Margolis Shop continued to make Colonial reproductions of the highest quality. Between 1926 and 1950, the shop produced approximately 7,400 pieces of furniture. Margolis furniture is a very strong seller today. Figures 6–30 and 6–31 show work from the Margolis Shop.

Margolis also fostered the talents of other cabinetmakers, like Charles Post, who went on to form his own shop and to do fine work. Abraham Fineberg set up his shop in Hartford in 1932, having come from Lithuania in 1929. He and his son, Israel, produced high-quality custom-

(*Text continued on page 79*)

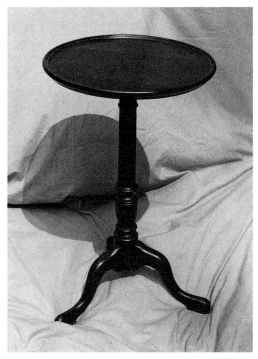

Fig. 6-7 Biggs c. 1940 dish-top candlestand, which sold for $15.50 around 1940. Very light weight. Three-board top. 15½″ diameter × 25″ high. *Private collection.* **$100–150.**

Fig. 6-8 Biggs c. 1930 Hepplewhite-style *demi-lune* card table with five legs, flip top, line inlays on frieze and on square, tapered legs. 36″ diameter × 30″ high. *Private collection.* **$400–600.**

Fig. 6-9 Biggs c. 1925–40 Queen Anne–style mahogany tea table. Rectangular top with raised thumb-molded edge, above a plain frieze, above an ogee serpentine apron. C-scrolled bordered knees, cabriole legs with pad feet, with two candle slides on either side. 30″ wide × 18½″ deep × 26½″ high. *Courtesy Frank H. Boos Gallery, Bloomfield Hills, Mich.* **$800–1,200.**

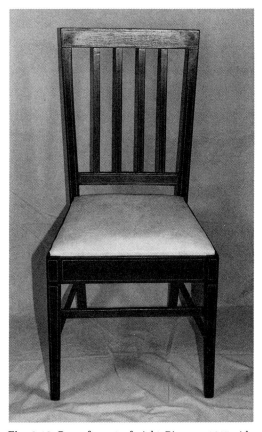

Fig. 6-10 One of a set of eight Biggs c. 1915 side dining chairs in Hepplewhite Revival style, with line inlays on chair back, seat rail, and legs. Chair back of dowel construction; legs are mortise-and-tenon joined. 18½″ wide × 17½″ deep × 38″ high. *Private collection.* **$2,400–3,600** the set.

Fig. 6-11 Biggs Hepplewhite-style c. 1915 round mahogany dining table with three leaves, line inlays. En suite with the dining chairs. 60″ diameter × 29¼″ high. *Private collection.* **$1,800–2,400.**

Fig. 6-12 Biggs Hepplewhite-style c. 1915 mahogany sideboard with slightly bowed front. Line inlays on front and on the six square, tapered legs. En suite with table and chairs. 72″ long × 28″ diameter × 40¼″ high. *Private collection.* **$1,200–1,800.**

76

Fig. 6-13 One of a set of eight Biggs c. 1910 solid mahogany Chippendale-style dining chairs (two arm chairs, six side chairs). Mortise-and-tenon construction, rear legs chamfered. Integral shoe, no molding on backsplat, stiles, or crest rail. Heavy in weight. Sides 20″ wide × 16½″ deep × 38½″ high. *Private collection.* **$2,400–3,600.**

Fig. 6-14 Biggs c. 1930–40 "Colonial" ottoman as described in the Biggs catalogue. 20″ long × 16″ wide. *Private collection.* **$75–115.**

Fig. 6-15 Biggs c. 1930 four-drawer Hepplewhite-style mahogany chest of drawers with French splay feet, oval brasses. Stringing around drawers. Top not molded—a lack of detail typical of Colonial Revival pieces. Top made of three boards, plywood back and drawer bottoms. 39¼″ wide × 20½″ deep × 38″ high. *Private collection.* **$800–1,200.**

Fig. 6-16 Biggs c. 1937 writing desk. The 1937 catalogue describes it as follows: "Late Sheraton mahogany writing table, with reeded legs. Reproduced from a period about 1760. 44″ long × 25″ deep × 40″ high overall, with two large drawers, three small drawers, two cupboards, and two letter boxes. $127.50." The description is not quite accurate. This is actually a reproduction of a c. 1800 style. The Biggs model has nailed drawers. *Private collection.* **$800–1,200.**

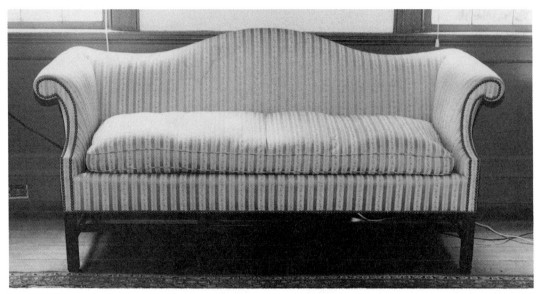

Fig. 6-17 Biggs c. 1938 Chippendale-style camelback sofa with single loose down cushion, on straight, molded legs. 80″ long × 32″ deep × 36″ high. *Private collection.* **$600–900.**

Fig. 6-18 Biggs c. 1938 Queen Anne–style wing chair with cabriole legs and pad feet. Back flares out nicely. 27½″ wide × 21½″ deep × 44″ high. *Private collection.* **$350–475.**

Fig. 6-19 Biggs c. 1938 Martha Washington–style mahogany chair. Very heavy and sturdy. 27″ wide × 26½″ deep × 24½″ high. *Private collection.* **$400–600.**

Fig. 6-20 Biggs c. 1930 Queen Anne–style wing chair. 34″ wide × 25″ deep × 40″ high. *Private collection.* **$175–275.**

Fig. 6-21 Biggs c. 1937 card table. From the 1937 catalogue: "Duncan Phyfe card table—has the typical reeded pedestal and reeded legs with brass claw feet. An impressive occasional table for use in Living Room, Dining Room, or Hall. Open, 36″ square, closed 18″ × 36″. Height 30″. Made of selected, solid mahogany with Biggs' dull antique finish. $75." *Private collection.* **$275–450.**

Fig. 6-22 Biggs c. 1937 armchair. From the 1937 catalogue: "Duncan Phyfe armchair of unusually graceful lines, has carved cross slat in back and is shaped to the back for comfort. Seat is filled with finest quality hair. This chair is justly popular because of its comfort and its appropriateness as an occasional chair, desk chair, or at the dining or bridge table. $35." *Private collection.* **$225–375.**

made reproductions that were often inspired by Lockwood's or Nutting's books. Fineberg adapted an original piece to suit the client's needs, which usually meant that the pieces were scaled down to accommodate lower ceiling heights. Fineberg generally did not mark his pieces. Post and Fineberg reproductions are eagerly sought today.

In Framingham, Massachusetts, Wallace Nutting continued making his high-quality reproductions during the 1930s. However, his business never fully recovered from the Depression; his business declined all through the 1930s, ending with his death in 1941.

There were many small shops around the country making reproductions of an-

Fig. 6-23 Biggs c. 1940 mahogany lowboy/desk of simple form. One long over two short cock-beaded drawers. Square, tapered legs. *Courtesy Whitehall at the Villa Antiques and Fine Art, Chapel Hill, N.C.* **$450–640.**

Fig. 6-24 Biggs c. 1920 Queen Anne–style settee with shell-carved knees, pad feet. 45½" long × 24" deep × 39" high. *Private collection.* **$1,800–2,400.**

tiques, often local pieces. These cabinetmakers did not market their reproductions beyond their locality. Instead, they made pieces to meet specific demands of local clients, who may have wanted a copy of a local antique. We all know of estate settlements in which one family member gets the fine eighteenth-century table, and the other family member gets an exact copy of the antique. These pieces were produced by local cabinetmakers all around the country, and still are today.

The Depression in general had a detrimental effect on the Colonial Revival movement. Most people could no longer afford to indulge their interest. However, if one did have money during the Depression, it was a great time to buy antiques, since people who normally would have cherished family heirlooms were forced to sell fine antiques. We know of one case in which a museum buying the family antique commissioned an exact copy for the owners! This must have happened often when museums, dealers, or private collectors purchased family pieces. No doubt, this type of transaction led to many fine local reproductions. It also led, no doubt, to those dubious and astounding stories dealers often encounter—of reproductions thought by owners to be real.

The furniture industry of the 1930s

Fig. 6-25 Biggs c. 1937 Sheraton-style four-poster bed. Headboard with acanthus-carved broken arch with rosette terminals and urn finial. Posts are reeded, with acanthus carving. 81½" long × 58" wide × 92" high. *Private collection.* **$1,800–2,600.**

Fig. 6-26 Valentine tilt-top tea table of mahogany, with chamfered underside, two-board top. Richmond, Virginia, c. 1925. 20" diameter × 30" high. Finish ruined. *Private collection.* **$125–175.**

Fig. 6-27 Valentine c. 1930 Queen Anne Revival wing chair with schematized, shell-carved knees, pad feet. Virginia walnut or mahogany. 48" high. H. C. Valentine Company catalogue, c. 1930. **$450–600.**

was hampered in the early years by the Depression, and at the beginning of the next decade by the entry of the United States into World War II. Naturally, with the gathering clouds of war and the lend-lease boom, large furniture factories turned their energies toward the war effort. Smaller cabinetmakers all around the country often disappeared into the armed forces. The entire furniture industry restructured to manufacture goods needed for the war. The Colonial Revival movement in furniture suffered as a result.

The Colonial Revival had been the focus of great national interest and was directed toward greater historical accuracy by the influential museum exhibits and the flamboyant collectors of the 1920s. By the end of the 1920s, all of the trends in Colonial Revival furniture were established: reproductions were available for all pocketbooks, including mass-produced pieces that took great liberties with

Fig. 6-30 Three of a set of twelve mahogany Chippendale-style chairs (ten side chairs and two arm chairs) with interlaced gothic splats, scrolled arms, and molded seat frames and front legs. Branded "Margolis 1929." From the Nathan Margolis Shop, Hartford, CT. *Courtesy Nadeau's Auction Gallery, Windsor, Conn.* **$8,000–12,000.**

Fig. 6-28 Valentine c. 1930 "Colonial" or Empire Revival dressing table and stool. Dresser has acanthus-carved standards and legs, three-over-two cock-beaded drawers. Mahogany and mahogany veneer. 48″ wide × 24″ deep × 71″ high. Stool is solid mahogany with acanthus-carved legs. 24″ wide × 15″ deep × 20″ high. H. C. Valentine Company catalogue, c. 1930. Dresser. **$500–750.** Stool, **$150–250.**

Fig. 6-29 Valentine c. 1930 Chippendale-style block-front, slant-lid desk with four graduated drawers, shell-carved apron, ball-and-claw feet, fitted interior. Solid mahogany. 42″ wide × 22″ deep × 42″ high. H. C. Valentine Company catalogue, c. 1930. **$500–800.**

Fig. 6-31 Queen Anne–style c. 1937–41 mahogany highboy, with broken-arch pediment, two fan carvings, cyma carved skirt, cabriole legs with pad feet. Branded: "Handmade by the Nathan Margolis Shop Hartford, Conn." *Courtesy Nadeau's Auction Gallery, Windsor, Conn.* **$1,800–2,400.**

style and attempted only to suggest a nostalgic past. The major museum exhibits of the 1920s validated early American furniture and design as a field worthy of collecting and scholarship. These exhibits also led to more accurate, higher-quality reproductions. After the Great Depression, the Colonial Revival movement was no longer the center of national attention, as the country was diverted by the war and by rebuilding for peacetime. The new modernism caught on during this era and became central to large factory production, as did the use of new materials arising from wartime production. Colonial styles continued to be produced and a few museums began to formalize their reproductions, providing the public with a source of good-quality reproductions. Certainly by the end of the 1930s the Colonial Revival movement had successfully established Colonial styles as a mainstay of the furniture industry that prevails even today.

PART II

Furniture Forms and Prices

7

Chairs and Sofas

William and Mary or "Flemish"-style c. 1910–20 oak side chair with applied half-spindles on the stiles, spindle arcades showing influence of Spanish design, carved top and lower rails, block-turned front legs, spool-turned front stretcher. Needlepoint seat. Mortise-and-tenon joints, a sign of high-quality workmanship. Probably made in New York City. 19″ wide × 17¼″ deep × 40″ high. *Private collection.* **$175–275.**

One of a pair of c. 1910 tall, dramatic Jacobean-style open armchairs with strong sweeping arms hand-carved with acanthus leaves curling under at knuckles. Barley-twist stretchers. Arched and shaped backs. Beautiful old needlework. The somewhat exaggerated arms and the poorly proportioned bun feet are out of character and lower the value of this chair. 27¼″ wide × 19¼″ deep × 53″ high. *Courtesy Reynolda House, Museum of American Art, Winston-Salem, N.C.* **$1,500–2,000,** single. **$3,000–4,000,** the pair.

Cromwellian-style c. 1920 oak open armchair with barley-twist legs and stretchers, scrolled arms with acanthus carving. Needlepoint seat and back. 24½" wide × 26" deep × 38½" high. *Courtesy Chameleon Antiques, Newport News, Virginia* **$325–475.**

William and Mary–style c. 1920 cane-back side chair with double-scroll front legs and scrolling underbracing. Block-turned rear legs and stretchers. Worn needlepoint seat. 20½" wide × 19" deep and 49½" high. *Courtesy Chameleon Antiques, Newport News, Virginia.* **$400–600,** single. **$900–1,500** the pair.

Open armchair, c. 1910, with out-curving arms ending in spiral turns. Front legs ending in hoof feet. Upholstered back and seat in old needlepoint. Knees with rosette terminals, acanthus and bellflower carving, beaded rim above hoof feet. Strong legs, weak arms, low back. 24½" wide × 17" deep × 36" high. *Courtesy Reynolda House, Museum of American Art, Winston-Salem, N.C.* **$800–1,200** (high price due to needlework).

Jacobean-style c. 1910 straight-back open armchair with curving arms ending in spiral terminals. Legs and stretchers are block-turned. This typical adaptation does not retain the vigor of the original chair. 25″ wide × 21½″ deep × 44″ high. *Courtesy Reynolda House, Museum of American Art, Winston-Salem, N.C.* **$100–175.**

William and Mary–style c. 1920 factory-made hall chair with caned back and seat, carved crest rail, turned stretchers. Refinished. 22″ wide × 18″ deep × 54″ high. *Collection of Naomi and Norman Ludwig.* **$600–900.**

Pair of c. 1930 William and Mary/Spanish-style walnut medallion-carved side chairs with stretcher bases. Stiles and backs are carved. 35″ high. *Private collection.* **$400** the pair.

Jacobean-style c. 1920 open armchair with barley-twist stretchers, supports, and arms. Arms end in wonderful hand-carved recumbent lions. 25½" wide × 20½" deep × 37½" high. *Courtesy Reynolda House, Museum of American Art, Winston-Salem, N.C.* **$800–1,200.**

Queen Anne transitional-style lolling chair, c. 1910, with shepherd's-crook arms and ball-and-claw feet. Knees with C-scroll carving. Upholstered back and seat. Philadelphia. *Private collection.* **$600–900.**

Sheraton-style c. 1900 open armchair. *Courtesy Reynolda House, Museum of American Art, Winston-Salem, N.C.* **$400–600.**

Sheraton-style c. 1900 mahogany open armchair or lolling chair with wheat carving. Reeded and turned front legs, on rollers, reeded arms. 21″ deep × 47″ high. *Private collection.* **$500–700.**

Stretcher-based lolling chair, c. 1910, with shaped apron, cabriole legs. Pad feet in front, straight legs in rear. Curving arms with scroll terminals. Upholstered back and seat. *Private collection.* **$450–650.**

Fireside pull-up chair, c. 1920, in the Chippendale style. Mahogany legs. 25″ wide × 23″ deep × 35″ high. *Courtesy Chameleon Antiques, Newport News, Virginia* **$300–475.**

Rocking chair, c. 1890–1900, showing the influence of Chippendale with its pierced splat. A far cry from eighteenth-century Chippendale, we would call this a Colonial Revival adaptation of Chippendale. Found in oak, mahogany, mahoganized cherry or birch. *Private collection.* **$175–275.**

Sheraton-style racket-back child-size rocking chair with needlepoint seat. Splat broken. The rocking chair was especially popular as an adaptive Colonial Revival form. *Private collection.* As is, **$100–150.** Perfect **$350–450.**

Adapted Sheraton Revival–style armchair, c. 1905–20, with line inlay on crest rail and arms. Doweled construction, mahogany. 22″ wide × 19″ deep × 30¼″ high. *Private collection.* **$175–325.**

Child's Windsor-style rocking chair with turned arm supports and legs, c. 1920. Labeled "J. B. Van Sciver Co. Camden, N.J." *Private collection.* **$100–150.**

American walnut slat-back Empire Revival–style rocker, c. 1900. 21½″ wide × 19″ deep × 37⅛″ high. *Private collection.* **$150–250.**

Open armchair, c. 1895–1905, with mother-of-pearl inlay and applied acanthus carving on crest rail, pierced splat. Spindles and legs show a Sheraton influence. Mahogany or mahoganized native woods. 24½″ wide × 17¾″ deep × 35½″ high. *Private collection.* **$275–475.**

Pastiche window seat/armchair with caned seat, applied carvings on crest rail and arms, odd little splat, shaped apron, and front stretchers. Factory made, c. 1910. *Private collection.* **$175–275.**

Sheraton Revival side chair, c. 1900, with reeded stiles, line inlay and pattera on crest rail, stringing on tapered front legs. Doweled construction, mahogany. 19″ wide × 15¾″ deep × 36″ high. *Private collection.* Single, **$175–275.** Set of six (two plus four), **$1,800–2,700.** Set of eight (two plus six) **$3,200–4,200.**

Hepplewhite Revival–style mahogany fan-back side chair of doweled construction. 22″ wide × 19″ deep × 30¼″ high. *Private collection.* Single, **$100–175.** Set of six (two arm chairs, four side chairs), **$1,500–2,400.** Set of eight (two armchairs, six side chairs), **$3,000–4,000.**

Underside of one of the dining chairs (*opposite page, bottom*) showing the label for Moser Furniture Company.

Open armchair, c. 1900, in a Duncan Phyfe design after the English Regency. The flatness of the sides of the legs is indicative of factory work and depresses the value of this otherwise fine Colonial Revival chair. *Private collection.* **$300–450.**

One of a set of four c. 1920 Empire-style dining chairs made by Moser Furniture Company of Lynchburg, Virginia. The company was founded in 1915 and sold bench-made reproductions using hand-dovetailing, mortising, hand carving, and good-quality woods. Each chair is labeled. Note the urn-shaped splat. In the late nineteenth century these chairs would have been called "Grecian" in style. 18″ wide × 17″ deep × 33″ high. *Private collection.* **$500–750** set of four.

Sheraton-style c. 1900 lyre-back side chair with acanthus-leaf and other carving on back, turned and reeded front legs. Doweled construction. Back legs of glued-up stock. 19¼″ wide × 18″ deep × 32¼″ high. *Private collection.* **$150–225.**

One of a set of eight (two armchairs, six side chairs) dining chairs, c. 1905, combining Queen Anne with other stylistic elements. Crinoline stretchers. 19½″ wide × 17½″ deep × 39½″ high (sides). *Private collection.* **$1,600–2,400** the set.

Sheraton-style c. 1900 lyre-back side chair with up-holstered back and seat, turned and reeded front legs. Doweled construction. Back legs of glued-up stock. 20″ wide × 18¼″ deep × 33½″ high. *Private collection.* **$375–550** for a pair.

One of a set of six (two armchairs, four side chairs) Chippendale-style c. 1900 solid mahogany ladder-back dining chairs with straight legs and well-carved interlaced back supports. Arms rather poorly shaped. Rear legs of glued-up stock. 20″ wide × 18¾″ deep × 39″ high (sides). *Private collection.* **$1,200–1,800** the set.

One of a set of eight (two armchairs, six side chairs) Sheraton-style dining chairs made by Tiffany Studios, 1915. Cuban mahogany. Molded back and arms, reeded and turned front legs. 19½″ wide × 18″ deep × 38″ high (sides). *Private collection.* In 1915, Tiffany sold the side chairs for $20 and the armchairs for $25. Today they are valued at **$75–125** (side) and **$175–275** (arm).

Elaborately carved Chippendale-style c. 1890 mahogany corner chair. Hand-carved, with swags, flowers, and scrolling foliage. Pierced backsplats similarly carved. Backsplats are silhouetted, an unusual touch on chairs of this date and a sign of quality workmanship. Arms are leaf-carved, as are stiles and three legs. Front leg is cabriole, with ball-and-claw foot. The elaborate carving is a good example of an exuberant Victorian interpretation of a typically more restrained Chippendale design. 17¾" × 17¾" × 23¾" high. *Private collection.* **$1,200–1,800.**

Solid mahogany c. 1900 bench-made corner chair in the Chippendale style with front cabriole leg ending in a ball-and-claw foot. Other legs are chamfered. Turned uprights, molded arms, pierced splats. *Private collection.* **$800–1,200.**

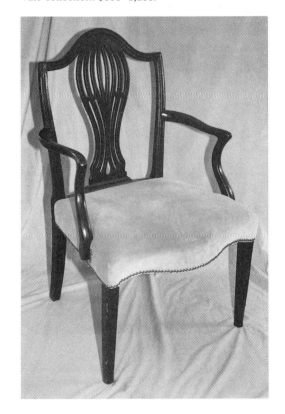

Single c. 1925 Hepplewhite-style mahogany armchair with molded back and front legs, shaped arms. Good form and quality mahogany. *Courtesy Reynolda House, Museum of American Art, Winston-Salem, N.C.* **$300–450,** single. **$800–1,200** the pair.

Chippendale-style c. 1900 mahogany ladder-back or ribbon-back armchair with needlepoint seat. Light weight, small size. Curving seat rail is a nice touch. Stiles are molded; otherwise, arms and legs are devoid of any carving. This example is somewhat battered. *Private collection.* **$350–500.**

Chippendale-style chairs in the gothic taste were manufactured in many versions around the turn of the century. Collectors should be discriminating and look only for the best. This chair is a basic mahogany c. 1910 Chippendale-style side chair with a pierced gothic splat and cabriole legs ending in well-articulated ball-and-claw feet. It is otherwise devoid of carving. *Private collection.* **$300–450,** side chair. **$600–900,** arm-chair. Set of eight, **$4,500–6,000.**

Nicely proportioned Chippendale-style side chair with pierced and molded gothic splat, shell carving on seat rail, acanthus carving on knees, ball-and-claw front feet. Needs to be refinished. Baltimore, c. 1915. *Private collection.* **$400–600.**

An interesting, rather outlandish pair of c. 1880–1920 Chippendale-style mahogany chairs (six side chairs and two armchairs). Carved crest rails with ears, backsplats with scrolling entwined snakes, fleur-de-lys (an odd combination). The arms have snake ends curving inward. Gadrooned seat rails, acanthus knees, well-articulated ball-and-claw feet. What these chairs lack in unity of design, they make for in visual interest. *Courtesy Richard Beecher.* **$8,000–12,000** the set.

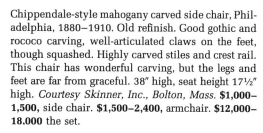

Chippendale-style mahogany carved side chair, Philadelphia, 1880–1910. Old refinish. Good gothic and rococo carving, well-articulated claws on the feet, though squashed. Highly carved stiles and crest rail. This chair has wonderful carving, but the legs and feet are far from graceful. 38″ high, seat height 17½″ high. *Courtesy Skinner, Inc., Bolton, Mass.* **$1,000–1,500,** side chair. **$1,500–2,400,** armchair. **$12,000–18.000** the set.

Chippendale-style c. 1920 side chair with shell-carved crest rail, pierced backsplat. Rear legs chamfered, shaped apron, front cabriole legs with ball-and-claw feet. large size. Mahogany. Rather stiff back. 22″ wide × 17¼″ deep × 41¾″ high. *Private collection.* Single, **$300–450.** Set of six (two plus four), **$2,400–3,600.** set of eight (two plus six), **$4,800–6,500.**

Chippendale-style c. 1890–1910 armchair of mahogany in the Philadelphia manner. Acanthus carving on the knees and applied shell on the straight seat rail. The arms are shaped, with knuckle terminals. The arms are slightly contoured rather than flatly horizontal. *Private collection.* **$400–600,** side chair. **$700–1,000** armchair. Set of eight, **$6,000–10,000.**

A similar Chippendale-style c. 1890–1910 mahogany armchair in the Philadelphia manner with gothic splat. Proportions are squatter. The arms have no contouring on the horizontal axis. legs are thicker and stockier, squarish. Applied shell on straight seat rail. Acanthus carved knees, ball-and-claw feet. Carving on legs and feet is flat and schematic. The shaping of the legs is not complete; the legs are not fully rounded. This is part of a set of eight (two plus six) dining chairs. *Private collection.* **$6,000–10,000** the set.

This side chair is similar, but the proportions are better. The shape and curve of the legs are closer to the grace of the eighteenth-century original. The shaped seat rail adds grace. The mahogany is of a better quality and a heavier weight than the last set. However, one should not mistake this for an eighteenth-century chair. Some clues indicate that this is Colonial Revival (the applied shell on the seat rail is not a rococo shell. It is long and pendulous—a late nineteenth-century interpretation of rococo). We had a chance to turn this chair upside down and found circular-saw marks under the seat rail and band-saw marks on the underside of the shell, tools not used in eighteenth-century America. **$500–700.**

Armchair from the same set as the preceding side chair. The set consists of two arms and six sides. **$500–700,** side chair. **$800–1,200,** armchair. **$8,000–12,000** the set.

One of a set of six c. 1880 transitional Chippendale side chairs with pierced splats and "bird" backs, rush seats, block-turned front legs, Spanish feet, bulbous-turned front stretchers. 18¼" wide × 15" deep × 39½" high. From a small shop. *Private collection.* Set of six, **$1,800–2,400.**

Chippendale Revival–style c. 1920 armchair with shell-carved knees and pad feet. Not true to period forms. 29½" wide × 20" deep × 39" high. *Courtesy Reynolda House, Museum of American Art, Winston-Salem, N.C.* **$300–450.**

Queen Anne–style c. 1930 armchair with pad feet and shell-carved knees. Walnut legs. True to early forms, except back is too short and arms are too thick. 34½" wide × 25¼" deep × 38¼" high. *Private collection.* **$400–600.**

Queen Anne–style c. 1900 mahogany wing chair with heavy, rather straight back legs. 28½″ wide × 22″ deep × 43″ high. *Private collection.* **$400–600.**

Chippendale-style c. 1915 wing chair with straight, molded legs and stretcher base. 32″ wide × 20″ deep × 41″ high. *Private collection.* **$450–650.**

Chippendale-style c. 1900 wing chair with short cabriole legs and ball-and-claw feet. 28″ wide × 22″ deep × 43½″ high. *Private collection.* **$500–750.**

Pair of c. 1920 Chippendale-style mahogany open armchairs, each with upholstered back, seat, and arm rests. Acanthus-carved handrests and arms. Carved. scrolled apron on cabriole legs. Acanthus-carved knees and feet. *Courtesy Leslie Hindman Auctioneers, Chicago.* **$3,000–4,500** the pair.

Chippendale-style c. 1930 carved mahogany wing chair with arched back and rolled arms. Cabriole legs with acanthus- and cabochon-carved knees and whorl feet. Fat arms, poor crest rail, good legs. *Courtesy Leslie Hindman Auctioneers, Chicago.* **$1,000–1,500.**

Empire Revival c. 1890 loveseat and armchair. Backs, seats, and rear backs upholstered. Winged paw feet, scrolled arms, carved crest rail. Cherry, now with black lacquer. Doweled construction. 53¾" long × 23" deep × 37" high. *Collection of Naomi and Norman Ludwig.* **1,200–1,800** the set.

Empire Revival armchair matching the loveseat.

Modified wing chair in the Chippendale style, c. 1920. Machine carving, doweled construction. 28½" wide × 24½" deep × 34" high. *Private collection.* **$400–600.**

Empire Revival c. 1890 armchair and settee of mahogany and mahogany veneer. Armchair with lion's paw feet (missing applied decoration), scrolling acanthus carving on arms and crest rail. 39″ wide × 20½″ deep × 32¼″ high. Settee with back crest sides of carved cornucopia and flowers, with winged lion's paw feet. 79″ long × 28″ deep × 34″ high. *Courtesy New Orleans Auction Galleries, New Orleans.* Chair, **$350–475.** Settee, **$750–1,200.**

Jacobean Revival c. 1920 sofa with triple-curved back, turned legs and stretchers. Found in mahogany, oak, and maple. 76″ long × 21½″ deep × 39″ high. *Courtesy Reynolda House, Museum of American Art, Winston-Salem, N.C.* **$800–1,500.**

Sofa en suite with the armchair *below*. 72″ long × 21″ deep × 38¾″ high. *Private collection.* **$800–1,200.**

Empire Revival c. 1890 armchair of mahogany veneer. Scrolled crest rails, cartouche backs, gadrooned seat rails, paw feet. These massive pieces were popular in the 1890s, when factories produced three-piece suites for the living room. These two pieces at one time may have had a matching rocker. Suites were often in a heavy, Empire style, but this one, interestingly enough, combines Empire with Queen Anne, Chippendale, and Adam features—an indication of the early Colonial Revival misunderstanding of historic design periods. This is as wild as it gets, folks! Chair is 40½″ wide × 21″ deep × 38½″ high. *Private collection.* **$350–475.**

Sheraton Revival c. 1900 factory-made settee with cabriole legs, applied ribbon and floral decoration. 42½″ long × 20″ deep × 29″ high. *Private collection.* **$350–550.**

109

William and Mary–style c. 1920 sofa with turned legs and stretchers. A rather odd adaptation, but in leather, and very comfortable. *Courtesy Reynolda House, Museum of American Art, Winston-Salem, N.C.* **$800–1,200.**

Chippendale-style c. 1900 camelback sofa of good proportions. Ball-and-claw feet, boldly carved, with shell knees. Down cushion, fine fabric. 82″ long × 23″ deep × 32½″ high. *Private collection.* **$600–900.**

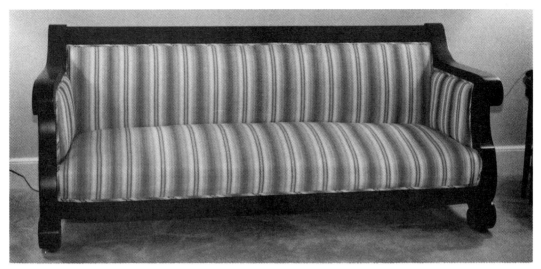

Empire Revival c. 1910 sofa with scrolled arms and feet of solid mahogany. During the Colonial Revival period, this sofa would have been called "Colonial" or "Empire Colonial." 77½" long × 28" deep × 32" high. *Private collection.* **$450–750.**

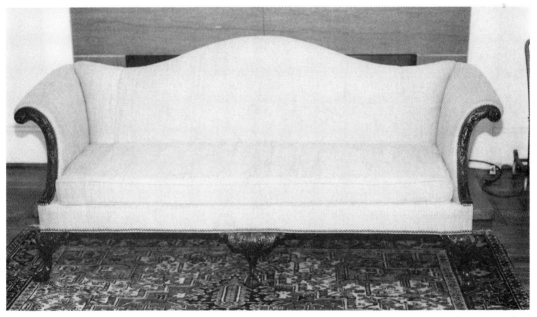

Camelback sofa, c. 1880–1900, with carved mahogany arm supports and cabriole legs with ball-and-claw feet. Richly carved mahogany arms and legs. Very good quality. *Private collection.* **$3,000–4,500.**

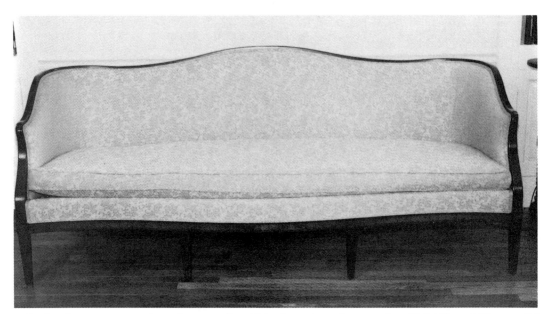

Federal-style c. 1920 serpentine mahogany sofa, with burl panels on the seat rail and inlaid legs. 84″ long × 23″ deep × 32″ high. *Private collection.* **$1,800–2,400.**

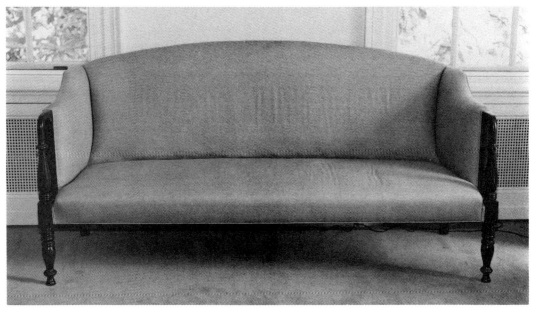

Sheraton-style c. 1915 sofa. Legs are not well turned and are bulky. *Courtesy Reynolda House, Museum of American Art, Winston-Salem, N.C.* **$600–900.**

Federal-style c. 1920 mahogany and figured maple veneer sofa, made in Portsmouth, New Hampshire. Reeded and turned arms and front legs. 79″ long × 36″ high. *Courtesy Skinner, Inc., Bolton, Mass.* **$1,200–1,800.**

Chippendale-style c. 1900 solid mahogany camelback sofa with straight, molded legs, molded base trim and returns, and stretcher base. Down cushion. 84″ long × 21″ deep × 36½″ high. *Private collection.* **$800–1,200.**

William and Mary–style c. 1920 kidney-shaped fireside seat with three caned panels, black lacquer. 54″ long × 12¾″ deep × 12″ high. *Collection of Naomi and Norman Ludwig.* **$400–600.**

Chippendale-style c. 1920 footstool with strongly turned handles, ball-and-claw feet, shaped apron, needlepoint covering. 20″ long × 9″ deep × 7¾″ high. *Courtesy Reynolda House, Museum of American Art, Winston-Salem, N.C.* **$60–90.**

8

Tables, Lowboys, and Stands

Factory-made trestle-based table, c. 1930, with molded top and turned legs. Labeled "French Trade mark, Minneapolis." 24″ wide × 14⅛″ deep × 22½″ high. *Private collection.* **$125–165.**

Tea cart or tea wagon, c. 1920. From 1890 to World War II in mahogany, strained soft woods, and mahoganized cherry or birch, and in all style periods. *Private collection.* **$225–325.**

Spider-leg gateleg table, c. 1920, possibly by Hungate, Schmeig, and Kotzian of New York City. 25¾″ long × 12″ deep × 27″ high. *Private collection.* **$275–475.**

Rococo-style c. 1915 boldly carved ashtray stand with triangular base, button feet, acanthus carving, cabochons. Usually in oak or walnut. 27¾" high. *Courtesy Reynolda House, Museum of American Art, Winston-Salen, N.C.* **$150–225**

Well-turned ashtray stand, c. 1915. Tripod base with beading and acanthus carving, spiral turning. Paw feet. Usually found in oak or walnut, sometimes in mahogany. 28¼" high. *Courtesy Reynolda House, Museum of American Art, Winston-Salem, N.C.* **$125–175.**

Late nineteenth-century Sheraton Revival mahogany nest of four tables with molded tops and "bamboo"-turned legs. *Private collection.* **$900–1,200.** These tables can be found in more ornate styles with fine veneers and inlays at **$1,800–2,400.**

Small sofa or side table, c. 1915, with trestle base and turned stretchers and legs. Top is a shaped oval with raised, molded edge with book-matched veneers. This is an adaptation of an earlier style to modern use. 21½″ long × 16″ wide × 23″ high. *Courtesy Reynolda House, Museum of American Art, Winston-Salem, N.C.* **$145–225.**

Jacobean-style c. 1920 oak tavern table or joint stool with turned legs and molded stretchers and frieze. Pegged, but top also secured with screws. 18″ long × 8½″ wide × 18″ high. *Private collection.* **$145–275.**

Jacobean- or Flemish-style c. 1915 triangular table with veneered top and double C-scroll legs, molded and shaped stretchers, bun feet. Frieze with pierced scroll and floral carving, carved with a band saw. 19″ sides, 23″ high. *Courtesy Reynolda House, Museum of American Art, Winston-Salem, N.C.* **$175–225.**

Small c. 1920 side table. Lifting lid has elaborate and delicate marquetry and burl panels. Thin legs end in pad feet. Burl veneer and line inlays all around frieze. A weak adaptive form. 16¼" long × 11" deep × 26¼" high. *Courtesy Reynolda House, Museum of American Art, Winston-Salem, N.C.* **$125–175.**

Brass-galleried two-tier dumbwaiter, c. 1915, with striking exotic wood veneers, edged in contrasting wood. Tripod base with slipper feet. 16" diameter × 25½" high. *Courtesy Reynolda House, Museum of American Art, Winston-Salem, N.C.* **$145–225.**

Kidney-shaped side table, c. 1915, with burl veneer top, brass gallery, and one hung drawer. Brass-galleried middle shelf. Trestle base. 37¾" long × 18½" deep × 30" high. *Courtesy Reynolda House, Museum of American Art, Winston-Salem, N.C.* **$275–375.**

William and Mary Revival c. 1915 walnut center table with round top with panels of burl and geometric inlay. Trumpet-turned legs and curving stretchers. Shaped, lipped apron. A scaled-down adaptation. 36" diameter × 28½" high. *Courtesy Reynolda House, Museum of American Art, Winston-Salem, N.C.* **$500–750.**

Transitional William and Mary/Queen Anne–style c. 1915 six-sided table with centered underbracing. Legs turned and eight-sided, ending in whorl feet. Top with six inset burl panels. 29½″ × 29½″ × 24″ high. Found in oak or mahogany. *Courtesy Reynolda House, Museum of American Art, Winston-Salem, N.C.* **$450–650.**

Elizabethan-style c. 1915 oak console table with shaped top, apron with pierced scroll carving. Laminated legs with bulbous turnings. Molded stretcher base. Conspicuous square pegs on the front of the piece, but a closer look reveals dowels. 38″ long × 18½″ deep × 29½″ high. *Courtesy Reynolda House, Museum of American Art, Winston-Salem, N.C.* **$400–600.**

Jacobean-style c. 1930 flip-top, gateleg games table (the entire top flips up) of curly walnut and tulip poplar. Turned legs, ball feet. Octagonal top is molded. 30⅜″ × 30⅜″ × 28″ high. *Private collection.* **$150–225.**

119

Hepplewhite-style c. 1930 Pembroke table with leather inset top. One real and one false drawer. Tapered legs end in brass casters. Mahogany crossbanded in satinwood. 29⅞" long × 18" wide × 27½" high. *Private collection.* **$400–600.**

Two-drawer stand of mahogany, maple, and cherry, c. 1900. Cock-beaded drawers with handmade dovetails. Square, tapered legs. 20¾" wide × 18¾" deep × 28¾" high. *Courtesy Whitehall at the Villa Antiques and Fine Art, Chapel Hill, N.C.* **$500–750.**

Tilt-top table, c. 1880, with scalloped, molded top, bird cage, flattened ball-and-claw feet. 31" diameter × 28½" high. *Courtesy Reynolda House, Museum of American Art, Winston-Salem, N.C.* **$800–1,200.**

Federal-style c. 1930 tiger maple candlestand with three spider legs, rather crude turnings on shaft. 16" × 16" × 29½" high. *Courtesy Whitehall at the Villa Antiques and Fine Art, Chapel Hill, N.C.* **$200–300.**

Factory-made round mahogany dish-top table, c. 1900, with turned baluster pedestal with acanthus-leaf carving, tripod base with drop finial, ending in laminated lion's paw feet. Refinished. Legs are schematized and two-dimensional rather than fully rounded. *Private collection.* **$175–275.**

Acanthus carving on pedestal. Note how shallow and schematized the machine carving is; hand-carving is much deeper and crisper.

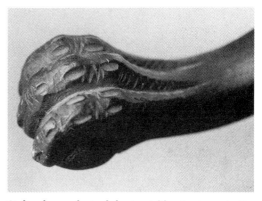

Stylized paw foot of the tea table. Again, note the shallow machine carving, only touched up by hand. Carving done completely by hand would have more depth and detail.

Underside of the dish-top table. The top is stamped with a model number (manufacturer unknown). Note the bottom of the lion's paw feet, with laminated wood added for necessary width. Top made of five boards.

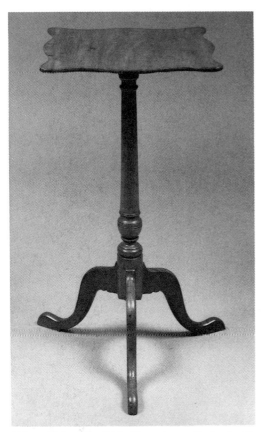

Late nineteenth-century mahogany Hepplewhite-style five-leg *demi-lune* card table with line inlay. Tapered legs end in cuffed feet. Refinished. Probably from Maryland. 36″ diameter × 30″ high. *Private collection.* **$800–1,200.**

Chippendale-style 1920–40 maple candlestand with serpentine square top over turned pedestal support and three down-curving legs, slipper feet. 16″ × 16″ × 27½″ high. *Courtesy Leslie Hindman Auctioneers, Chicago.* **$250–350.**

Hepplewhite-style c. 1900 mahogany *demi-lune* card table with various line inlays. Five tapered legs and cuffed feet. 35½″ diameter × 30⅜″ high. *Private collection.* **$800–1,200.**

Hepplewhite-style c. 1890 serpentine front flip-top games or tea table of mahogany with elaborate inlays. Apron with curly maple panels inset with marquetry. From Virginia area, bench-made. 35¾″ long × 17¾″ deep × 31″ high. *Private collection.* **$900–1,500**.

Hepplewhite-style c. 1930 five-leg *demi-lune* table with line inlays. Tapered legs with cuffed feet. Bench-made in a small cabinet shop in Raleigh, North Carolina. 36″ diameter × 29″ high. *Private collection.* **$800–1,400**.

Detail of the marquetry on the frieze of the tea table. The floral style is typical of 1890s work.

Chippendale-style c. 1910 square tea table with intricate shell-and-leaf carvings applied to the blocked center and ends on the skirt and gadrooned skirting fitting over the legs and around the corners, with no break. Laminated legs with carved knees and ball-and-claw feet. This table is a copy of an original New York table featured in Luke Vincent Lockwood's *Colonial Furniture in America*, published in 1901. It is highly likely that this table would have been manufactured after that date. The original table does not have gadrooning on the top edge, or shell carving on the sides. This copy is a good example of the way Colonial Revival pieces lack the restraint of eighteenth-century designs. The decoration on Colonial Revival pieces is often overdone. 37¾" wide × 23¾" deep × 29" high. Poplar, pine and mahogany with mahogany veneers on top and skirt. *Courtesy Chesapeake Antique Center, Queenstown, Maryland.* **$2,400–3,600.**

Sheraton-style c. 1920 mahogany flip-top games table. The fifth leg draws out with a drawer for holding cards and chips. Shaped top with reeded edge, reeded and turned legs. Marked: "Elite Tables, Elite Furniture Company, Jamestown, NY." Elite Furniture Company, founded in 1909, specialized in living-room tables and other occasional pieces. 35⅞" wide × 17" deep × 28" high. *Private collection.* **$450–750.**

Chippendale-style c. 1920 carved mahogany lowboy in the Philadelphia manner. Molded-edge rectangular top above one long over three short thumb-molded drawers, flanked by fluted, canted lamb's-tongue corners. Cabriole legs with foliate-carved knees end in ball and claw feet. While this piece captures more of the spirit of eighteenth-century design than many, note the crude, shallow carving on the knees and the ungraceful apron. 34" long × 30½" high. *Courtesy Butterfield & Butterfield, San Francisco, Calif.* **$2,400–3,500.**

Magnificent Chippendale-style hand-carved lowboy after a Philadelphia prototype illustrated in Wallace Nutting's *Furniture Treasury*, 1928. Fully carved ends and front-carved quarter-columns. Crosshatching on leg and skirt is an unusual characteristic found on few Philadelphia lowboys or highboys. This piece copies the highest form of the Philadelphia Chippendale style. Handmade and beautifully carved. This piece probably was made after the publication of Wallace Nutting's book; it is possible that the maker had access to the original, as the copy is so well executed. Mahogany with chestnut and pine secondary wood. 33⅛″ wide × 20½″ deep × 30″ high. *Courtesy Chesapeake Antique Center, Queenstown, Maryland* **$3,000–4,500.**

Queen Anne–style c. 1930 tiger maple desk or lowboy with molded top and three-over-two drawers. Fluted quarter-columns, shaped apron, cabriole legs. Similar models sold at Wanamaker's (Philadelphia) in 1927 for $110. 41¾″ long × 19″ deep × 29″ high. *Collection of Naomi and Norman Ludwig.* **$450–600.**

Queen Anne–style c. 1920 library table with shaped and shell-carved apron, laminated legs. Refinished. 46″ wide × 29″ deep × 30″ high. *Collection of Diana L. Altman.* **$400–600.**

Chippendale-style c. 1910 mahogany partner's desk with two-over-two drawers on two sides, gadrooned top, shaped and carved apron, cabriole legs with acanthus carving and ball-and-claw feet. Made with a combination of machine and hand work. Dovetails on drawers are handmade, but the carving is flat and lacks depth, typical of machine-made Colonial Revival carving. Top constructed of four boards, probably roughed out by machine and finished by hand. Cast brasses. 53¼″ long × 29¾″ deep × 30½″ high. *Private collection.* **$1,200–1,800.**

Chippendale-style c. 1910 mahogany writing desk with gadrooning around top, cabriole legs with acanthus-carved knees and ball-and-claw feet, corners with inset spiral-turned columns, ankles with exaggerated curves. This is a good example of a Colonial Revival piece using earlier design motifs but changing the proportions. Underside bears the label of Karcher and Rehm Company of Philadelphia. *Private collection.* **$1,200–1,800.**

Chippendale-style c. 1900 lowboy with molded top, cock-beaded drawers with handmade dovetails. Shaped apron on sides and front with applied rosette-type roundel—a typical Colonial Revival attempt to add some carving while saving the expense of handwork. Cabriole legs, ball-and-claw feet. 29¾″ wide × 19½″ deep × 30½″ high. *Courtesy Whitehall at the Villa Antiques and Fine Art, Chapel Hill, N.C.* **$900–1,600**

Handmade dish-top tea table, c. 1930, an exact copy of an original eighteenth-century table. Shows hand-tool marks. Cabriole legs with acanthus and bellflower carving. Vigorous ball-and-claw feet. Mahogany. 30⅜″ wide × 19⅛″ deep × 26⅜″ high. *Private collection.* **$1,800–2,600.**

Chippendale Revival c. 1900 mahogany dressing table with rectangular top with gadroon border above a single drawer, over leaf corner brackets with applied brass rosettes, flanked by rope-carved quarter-columns with brass capitals, supported on cabriole legs with shell-carved knees, ending in ball-and-claw feet. The legs and shell carving are sinewy and elongated. Flattened Victorian-type carving on frieze, topped off with rosettes, which have an Eastlake feeling. 34″ wide × 18″ deep × 32″ high. *Courtesy Osona Auction Gallery, Nantucket, Mass.* **$900–1,500.**

Chippendale-style c. 1920 mahogany lowboy with molded top over two-over-three-drawers. Central drawer with fan carving. Shaped apron, cabriole legs ending in ball-and-claw feet. 36″ wide × 20″ deep × 29″ high. *Private collection.* **$450–650.**

Queen Anne–style c. 1880 maple lowboy with molded top above long drawer over a central shell-carved drawer flanked by two drawers, on cabriole legs ending in pad feet. Handmade and handcarved. Top made of two boards. The stamped brasses look tinny. Pegged. Finish not original and in need of repair. Good proportions. 30½″ wide × 21″ deep × 31½″ high. *Courtesy Leslie Hindman Auctioneers, Chicago.* **$1,200–1,800.**

Queen Anne–style c. 1920 tea table with burl top and candle slides (oak), one cock-beaded drawer. Legs are solid walnut, pad feet, shell-carved knees. 33¼″ wide × 19½″ deep × 30″ high. *Private collection.* **$1,200–1,800.**

Queen Anne–style c. 1920 factory-made tea table with applied shells on front and back apron. Pad feet, cabriole legs. 27¾" long × 18" deep × 25¼" high. *Private collection.* **$600–900.**

Empire Revival–style flip-top table with one drawer, scroll feet, mahogany veneers. Purchased in Baltimore, 1915, when this piece would have been considered "Colonial" or "Empire Colonial." Empire Revival was popular with Baltimore furniture makers around the turn of the century. *Private collection.* **$175–275.**

Empire Revival–style c. 1910 library table with laminated scroll legs and feet. Mahogany veneers. One drawer. 49¾" long × 29½" deep × 28⅜" high. *Private collection.* **$300–475.**

William and Mary or Tudor-style c. 1900 oak buffet with bun feet, molded top, front with geometric panels of burl in fields of oak, with applied half-spindles. Dovetailed drawers with drop pulls. Three drawers over three cabinets. 71½″ wide × 24″ deep × 35¼″ high. *Courtesy Reynolda House, Museum of American Art, Winston-Salem, N.C.* **$1,500–2,400.**

Renaissance-style c. 1900 buffet with molded top over frieze with dentil carving. Three drawers with burl panels divided by acanthus scrolls. Drawers of oak, dovetailed. Front with four stop-fluted columns and three doors with burl panels. Gadrooned lower edge. Paw feet. 64″ long × 23¼″ deep × 39″ high. *Courtesy Reynolda House, Museum of American Art, Winston-Salem, N.C.* **$2,400–3,600.**

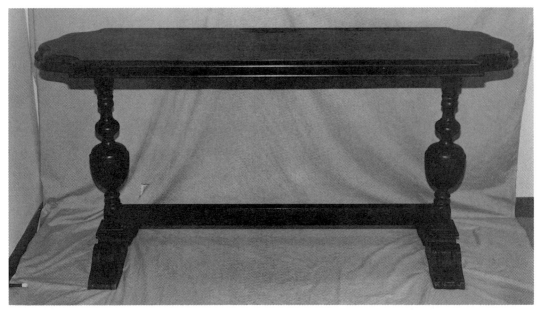

Jacobean-style c. 1920 factory-made refectory table with molded and shaped top, center stretcher base, turned supports with simple machine-carved fluting. Various woods. 61″ long × 19½″ deep × 28″ high. *Private collection.* **$300–475.**

William and Mary–style c. 1930 library table with molded top, three drawers, turned and fluted legs. Walnut and walnut veneers. 72″ long × 28″ deep × 30½″ high. *Private collection.* **$800–1,200.**

Hepplewhite-style c. 1940 walnut drop-leaf dining table with six square, tapered legs. Made by E. A. Clore and Sons, Madison, Virginia. 42⅛″ long × 20½″ deep × 29⅞″ high (leaves 20⅛″). *Private collection.* **$450–650.**

Regency-style c. 1925 inlaid mahogany sofa table, manufactured by Kittinger. The rectangular cross-banded top is flanked by two rounded drop leaves, over a frieze with two drawers and a trestle base joined by an upper stretcher on down-swept legs ending in brass casters. 32″ wide × 24″ deep × 29″ high. *Courtesy Leslie Hindman Auctioneers, Chicago.* **$900–1,200.**

Federal-style c. 1925 dining table with rectangular top and turned double-pedestal base, four down-curving legs ending in casters. With three leaves. A popular form copied throughout the twentieth century. 65″ long × 41¾″ wide × 30″ high. *Courtesy Leslie Hindman Auctioneers, Chicago.* **$2,400–4,800.**

Hepplewhite-style c. 1940 walnut single-drawer server, raised on tapered legs, en suite with the dining table (p. 133, top right) and chairs. Drawers with nailed construction. Made by E. A. Clore and Sons, Madison, Virginia. En suite with above table. 42½″ long × 20¼″ deep × 29⅞″ high. *Private collection.* **$225–325.**

Hepplewhite-style c. 1940 simple walnut sideboard with low backsplash, four graduated drawers flanked by two cabinets, on six turned legs. Labeled E. A. Clore and Sons, Madison, Virginia. 60⅛″ long × 20⅛″ deep × 39¼″ high. *Private collection.* **$800–1,200.**

Hepplewhite-style c. 1900 mahogany sideboard, the overall frame inlaid with rosewood, ebony, and satinwood bands. 74″ long × 30″ deep × 41″ high. *Courtesy Neal Auction Company, New Orleans.* **$1,200–2,400.**

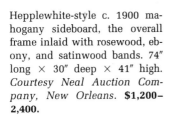

Hepplewhite-style c. 1900 round mahogany dining table with four leaves, satinwood line inlays on legs and frieze. On casters. From the Fredericksburg, Virginia, area. 54″ diameter × 30½″ high. *Private collection.* **$1,800–2,400.**

Hepplewhite-style c. 1900–1915 mahogany sideboard with bellflower inlays and patterae on cabinets. Plywood drawer bottoms and back, machine-made dovetails. 59½″ long × 21¾″ deep × 39″ high. *Private collection.* **$600–1,200.**

Hepplewhite-style c. 1900 sideboard, accurately styled. Mahogany with line inlays and flame veneers. *Courtesy Skinner, Inc., Bolton, Mass.* **$2,400–3,800.**

Jacobean Revival c. 1910 solid walnut stretcher-based serving table with drop leaves and gate legs. *Private collection.* **$500–750.**

Hepplewhite-style c. 1900 bench-made mahogany bow-front server with gallery back featuring pattera inlay. Line inlay on frieze and legs. Underside of bow front has blocks of wood glued to make the curve. From the Fredericksburg, Virginia, area. 52″ long × 21½″ deep × 28⅛″ high. *Private collection.* **$450– 650.**

Federal-style c. 1940 factory-made mahogany buffet with six drawers and two cabinets. Applied moldings, applied carving on canted corners, with fluting. Machine dovetails. 58⅜″ long × 18¾″ deep × 34½″ high. *Private collection.* **$250–475.**

Jacobean Revival c. 1920–30 solid walnut server or hall table with two full drawers flanked by two small drawers, raised on turned, stretchered legs. Applied half-spindles on front. 54″ long × 15¾″ deep × 37¾″ high. *Private collection.* **$500–750.**

9

Case Pieces, Beds, Clocks, and Oddities

Empire Revival c. 1910 mahogany pedestal sewing table with two drawers and drop leaves. Base with acanthus carving and paw feet. Drawers with nailed construction. A popular Colonial Revival piece. (Remember that around the turn of the century what we would normally refer to as Empire style was then called "Colonial" or "Empire Colonial.") 17⅜″ wide × 18″ deep × 29¾″ high. *Private collection.* **$175–275.**

Hepplewhite-style c. 1930 mahogany-veneered round end table with line inlay around top, sides, and drawers. Modified cabriole legs. Sides and top veneered. 20″ diameter × 27½″ high. *Private collection.* **$225–325.**

Martha Washington–style c. 1920 walnut sewing cabinet with lift-up top on central section fronted by three graduated drawers. Rounded, scalloped side sections have molded lift-up lids, scalloped bases. Cabriole legs with pad feet. This was a popular piece in the 1910s and 1920s. This particular example has several nice, unusual touches, especially the scalloping and cabriole legs. 27″ long × 13″ deep × 28″ high. *Collection of Diana L. Altman.* **$450–650.**

William and Mary–style c. 1915 sewing cabinet of Circassian walnut, by Tiffany Studios, New York City. Lift top, trumpet-turned legs, curving X-stretchers. 22″ long × 11″ deep × 28″ high. *Private collection.* **$500–750.**

Oak music cabinet, c. 1920, with door opening to reveal shelves for music or records. A popular, mass-produced item. *Courtesy Boulevard Bed and Breakfast, Wilmington, Del.* **$125–225.**

Dressing table, c. 1920, with two glove boxes, applied beading and carving. Square back legs, turned front legs. Dentilated trim on frieze. Machine-made dovetails on drawers. Applied carved scrolling on backsplash. 32″ wide × 20″ deep × 28⅞″ high. *Private collection.* **$115–175.**

Hepplewhite Revival c. 1920 mahogany Edison Victrola with tapered legs and brass cuffs. 18¾″ wide × 19½″ deep × 44¾″ high. *Private collection.* **$450–600.**

Factory-made lady's small desk, c. 1890, with fitted interior. Slant front has applied scrolls, typical of early c. 1890 Colonial Revival decoration. One central drawer with applied carving. Cabriole legs. Once had a backsplash. This type of desk was produced by large companies such as Paine's of Boston and by midwestern factories. Usually found in oak or mahogany. 41½″ wide × 16″ deep × 28″ high. *Collection of Diana L. Altman.* **$275–375.**

Small spinet desk of light mahogany, c. 1930, on turned legs, with writing slide and fitted interior. 32⅛″ wide × 18½″ deep × 32″ high. *Private collection.* **$250–450.**

Carved mahogany vanity c. 1890, with beveled glass mirror with scrolling carving flanked by scrolling stiles. Two glove drawers, shaped top, bow front with cock-beaded drawers, shaped and carved apron, cabriole legs with carved knees. Signed "R. J. Horner, N.Y." *Courtesy Southampton Antiques, Southampton, Mass.* **$800–1,200.**

Chippendale-style c. 1920 slant-front desk with oxbow front, during the Colonial Revival period often called a Governor Winthrop desk. Lupers extend automatically when slant-front is pulled down. Prospect door with pressed, carved fan. Ball-and-claw feet. *Private collection.* This kind of desk found in mahogany or stained soft wood. In mahogany, **$800–1,200.** In soft wood, **$450–675.**

George Washington writing table, c. 1920, modeled after one used by Washington in New York City. False drawers in back, working drawers in front, cockbeaded drawers, eight reeded legs, applied roundels. *Private collection.* **$800–1,250.**

Chippendale-style c. 1920 bench-made solid mahogany slant-front desk with two-over-two drawers. Fine fitted interior with three shells, blocked drawers. Ball-and-claw feet. Top of carcass with exposed dovetails. From the New York area. 37″ wide × 17″ deep × 40″ high. *Private collection.* **$600–900.**

Hepplewhite-style c. 1910 bench-made solid walnut chest of drawers. Carcass front and drawers with stringing, bracket feet. Walnut lightly figured. Drawers with handmade dovetails. 42″ wide × 44″ high. *Private collection.* **$500–750.**

Walnut veneered, adapted Chippendale-style cabinet, c. 1920, with molded top, ogee bracket feet. Doors with book-matched veneers and cross-banding. 36¼″ wide × 17½″ deep × 41½″ high. *Private collection.* **$600–900.**

Queen Anne–style c. 1930 mahogany chest of drawers with five graduated drawers. Molded top, inset reeded quarter-columns, shell-carved apron, cabriole legs, and pad feet. Drawers with machine-made dovetails. In the Colonial Revival era this would have been called a "Salem chest." 37¼″ wide × 20⅜″ deep × 38¼″ high. *Private collection.* **$400–600.**

Chippendale-style c. 1920 inlaid bow-front chest of drawers. Double stringing around drawer fronts. Molded, slightly bowed top, with conforming, graduated drawers. Awkward ball-and-claw feet. This piece is typical Colonial Revival in that it combines motifs from different design periods, in this case Federal-era stringing with Chippendale-style feet. *Courtesy Morton Goldberg Auction Galleries, New Orleans.* **$1,000–1,500.**

Factory-made c. 1920 Chippendale-style mahogany highboy of ordinary form, with little carving. Five graduated drawers in the top section over two graduated drawers in the lower part. Broken-arch pediment with turned finial and applied acanthus carving below. Shaped apron. Resting on cabriole legs with ball-and-claw feet. *Courtesy Motley's Auctions, Inc., Richmond, Virginia.* **$500–700.**

Chippendale-style inlaid mahogany highboy with three urn finials (finials missing) and broken-arch scrolled pediment with floral carving, over shell-carved center drawer flanked by two small drawers over four graduated drawers. Lower portion with one long drawer over one shell-carved drawer flanked by two small drawers over carved apron and cabriole legs with carved knees and pad feet. Drawers with cross-banding and line inlays. This example shows the flat carving often found on Colonial Revival pieces (even good ones like this), which is an easy tip-off for late nineteenth-century work. Flattened and more attenuated than good eighteenth-century carving (note especially the lines of the apron). 35″ wide × 19″ deep × 79″ high. *Courtesy Leslie Hindman Auctioneers, Chicago.* **$1,800–3,000.**

Chippendale-style c. 1880–1900 highly carved mahogany glazed-front bookcase. Pierced, scrolling, broken-arch pediment with rosette terminals. Blind-fret carving on door fronts. Legs and apron with shell carving, paw feet. 48″ wide × 15″ deep × 91½″ high. *Courtesy New Orleans Auction Galleries, New Orleans.* **$3,500–5,000.**

Chippendale-style c. 1900 mahogany chest-on-chest, a beautiful bench-made reproduction of a classic piece. Broken-arch bonnet top with three flame finials. Top section headed by shell-carved central drawer flanked by two short drawers over four long drawers. Lower section with two short drawers over three long drawers. Top and bottom with reeded, quarter-column case. Resting on ball-and-claw feet. Bat-wing brasses. 41″ wide × 18¼″ deep × 87″ high. *Courtesy Anthony J. Nard & Company, Milan, Penna.* **$3,500–4,800.** A good investment, especially considering that an eighteenth-century American piece of the same stylistic quality would cost over $100,000!

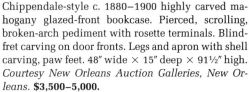

Chippendale-style mahogany chest-on-chest, in the manner of Newport, Rhode Island, another fine example of late nineteenth-century work. Scrolling broken-arch pediment with rosette terminals, three flame finials. Upper section with three aligned shell-carved drawers over four block-front graduated drawers with molded drawer openings. Lower section with four block-front graduated drawers, also with molded drawer openings. Conforming molded base, resting on ball-and-claw feet. Bat-wing brasses. 37″ wide × 21½″ deep × 6′8½″ high. *Courtesy William Doyle Galleries, New York City.* **$5,000–7,500.** A comparable eighteenth-century American piece would cost over $1 million.

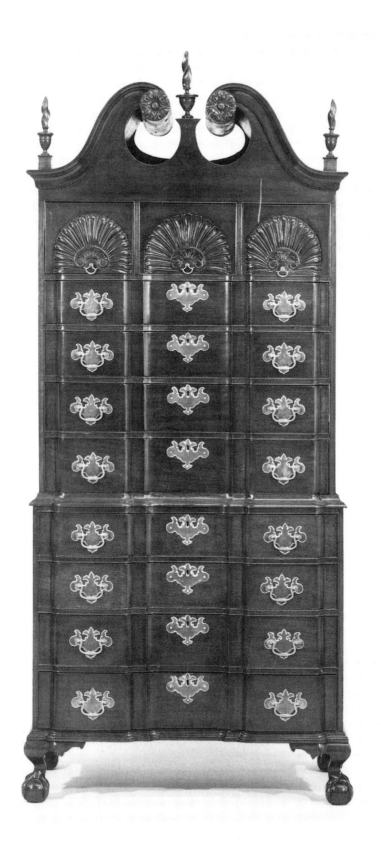

147

Chippendale-style c. 1880–1900 mahogany secretary bookcase. Broken-arch pediment of scaled-down proportions, with rosette terminals and acanthus carving, urn finial. Thirteen-pane glazed doors above slant-front lower section. Interior with serpentine drawers and compartments, shell-carved door flanked by columns with flame finials. Four long graduated drawers. Resting on squat ball-and-claw feet. 42½" wide × 21" deep × 92½" high. *Courtesy New Orleans Auction Galleries, New Orleans.* **$1,500–2,400.**

Chippendale-style c. 1900 mahogany secretary bookcase with broken-arch pediment mounted with three urn and flame finials and shell and acanthus carving; over a pair of mullion-glazed doors above fall-front writing surface, over block-front case with carved shells comprised of four drawers, on ball-and-claw feet. Inset, reeded quarter-columns. 43" wide × 22" doop × 94" high. *Courtesy Leslie Hindman Auctioneers, Chicago.* **$4,000 –6,000.**

Hepplewhite-style c. 1880–1900 secretary with two eight-pane doors enclosing shelves and fitted interior. Fold-out writing surface over four graduated cock-beaded drawers. Apron and cornice with inlay. French splay feet. *Courtesy Richard Beecher.* **$1,500–2,400.**

Seth Thomas c. 1920 mantel clock with molded top, gilded columns, rose-painted face, molded base. Features an image of Mount Vernon, much loved in the Colonial Revival era. 10¾″ wide × 5″ deep × 14¼″ high. *Private collection.* **$125–175.**

Carved oak tall-case clock, c. 1880–1900, probably by Walter H. Durfee and Company, Providence, Rhode Island. Broken-arch pediment (finials missing) over arched case flanked by rope-turned columns on all three parts of case. Shell carving above pendulum (missing). Paw feet. Moon phase. 8′ high. *Courtesy Skinner, Inc., Bolton, Mass.* **$3,000–5,000.**

Left: Tiffany and Company mahogany tall-case clock with gold and silver face beneath curved bonnet top supported by reeded columns. Original finish and presentation plaque. 24½″ wide × 16¼″ deep × 86″ high. **$4,000–6,000.** *Right:* Tiffany and Company tall-case clock, c. 1910. Iodized mahogany, with lion's paw feet, broken-arch pediment. 24½″ wide × 15″ deep × 97″ high. **$4,000–6,000.** *Courtesy New Orleans Auction Galleries, New Orleans.*

Similar to the clock at *right* on page 149, this is another c. 1880–1900 carved mahogany tall-case clock, by Walter H. Durfee and Company, Providence, Rhode Island, with carved, scrolled bonnet, three pairs of twisted columns with brass capitals and moon dial. 98½″ high. *Courtesy Rafael Osona, Nantucket, Mass.* **$3,000–4,500.**

Mahogany tall-case chiming clock, c. 1900, by Walter
H. Durfee and Company, Providence, Rhode Island.
Swan-neck pediment with three urn and flame finials, on a glazed case flanked by columns with capitals, shell carving above pendulum, gadrooning and
acanthus carving. Paw feet. Arched dial with painted
moon phase, silvered chapter and subsidiary rings,
chiming on eight tubes with Westminster and "Eight
Bells" chimes. 96" high. *Courtesy Northeast Auctions, Hampton, New Hampshire.* **$5,000–7,500.**

Roxbury-style c. 1920 mahogany tall-case clock with
Westminster chimes. Made by Bigelow and Kennard
Company, Boston. 7'6" high. *Courtesy Southampton
Antiques, Southampton, Mass.* **$3,500–5,500.**

Mahogany hourglass cheval mirror, c. 1900, applied leaf carvings. *Courtesy of Southampton Antiques, Southampton, Mass.* **$900–1,400.**

Tall-case clock of simple form with molded, arched bonnet, c. 1913. Face flanked by columns. Silent hour strike. Revolving landscape and seascape and two moons above clock face. Pendulum flanked by columns. Lion's paw feet. By H. Mahlor's Sons, Raleigh, North Carolina. 24¼″ wide × 14¼″ deep × 90¼″ high. *Private collection.* **$2,000–3,000.**

Mahogany four-poster bed, c. 1920, broken-arch headboard and footboard. Posts are reeded and carved with acanthus leaves and swags. 54" wide × 80" long. *Private collection.* **$225–425.**

Federal-style maple four-poster single bed, c. 1930–1940. High, turned posts with urn finials. *Courtesy of Neal Auction Company, New Orleans.* **$1,000–1,800,** pair.

POSTSCRIPT

We end this book with World War II because national attention had by then been diverted from the Colonial Revival movement—first by the Great Depression and, later, by the war. With returning soldiers interested in some of the styles they had seen abroad, the furniture industry had new postwar tastes to accommodate. The Colonial Revival began to settle into the familiar, ubiquitous style that we take for granted today. In 1993 we Americans seem to be just as interested in our past as ever, and we find Colonial designs all around us in the designs of our homes and furnishings. Colonial designs constitute a solid, dependable segment of the current furniture market, and it seems likely that they always will.

Probably the most important development in Colonial reproductions in the decades since World War II has been the increase in museum-sponsored reproduction programs that began in the 1930s. Reproductions from museum collections are generally more accurately styled than pieces commonly available in the Colonial Revival era, although museums also sponsor reproductions that adapt the original form to modern needs. The highest level of accuracy is found in the hallmarked pieces offered by several museums. These reproductions duplicate the primary and secondary wood of the original, along with many of the construction techniques. While there are certainly small custom shops making reproductions with even higher levels of hand

work, museum-licensed reproductions are more readily available and more widely marketed.

In 1936 Colonial Williamsburg licensed a line of English and American reproductions to be made by Kittinger of Buffalo, New York. Kittinger made high-quality reproductions, with a good deal of hand work and finishing. In 1991 Colonial Williamsburg contracted with Baker Furniture Company to continue and expand the line of reproductions that Kittinger had begun. There are now around thirty-three pieces from Colonial Williamsburg's collections being reproduced by Baker, with the highest level the hallmarked pieces. Most of the pieces are American in origin, with several from Virginia.

One example from the current Baker/Williamsburg catalogue shows a c. 1753 Philadelphia Chippendale-style high chest (or highboy) with cartouche-carved finial, scrolling pediment, flame finials, two shell- and acanthus-carved drawers, carved knees, cabriole legs, and ball-and-claw feet. It represents the highest caliber of eighteenth-century American design. According to the catalogue, the piece is made up of nearly four hundred parts, with two hundred ninety-eight hand-cut dovetails and hand carving. The catalogue also describes some of the construction techniques used in hallmarked pieces: hand-cut dovetails, mortise and tenon construction, floating panel construction, and stacked core surfaces. Other hallmarked pieces from this catalogue include a c. 1790 Norfolk, Virginia, serpentine chest with a floating panel back, a top made from a single board, inlaid chamfered corners and splay feet. There is a c. 1770 Philadelphia Rococo armchair and side chair, both with carved crest rail, fluted stiles, shell-carved apron, acanthus knees, ball-and-claw feet, and through mortise and tenon construction. Also included in the catalogue are a Philadelphia armchair with Marlborough legs; a c. 1750 Massachusetts tea table; a c. 1800 New England easy chair; a c. 1790 Virginia Pembroke table; and many other pieces. All are branded with the marks of Colonial Williamsburg and Baker. There are a number of lacquer finishes available to match the exact color of the original pieces. The finishes are largely done by hand.

The Henry Ford Museum in Dearborn arranged with Colonial Furniture Company of Zeeland, Michigan, to reproduce a number of pieces from the collection in the 1930s. This relationship continued until fairly recently. The Henry Ford Museum has been active in keeping up its reproduction program, with new efforts launched in the early 1960s, in 1975, and again in 1991. The American Life Collection debuted in 1991, featuring clocks made by Sligh Furniture Company of Holland, Michigan. Sligh currently makes four tallcase clocks for the Henry Ford Museum, based on originals by Jacob Eby, Joseph Doll, Thomas Harland, and Simon Willard. Sligh also makes a William Gilbert mantel clock and a Benjamin Morrill wall clock as part of the American Life Collection. The tallcase clocks apparently are scaled down for modern ceiling heights. Sligh promotional material describes the Doll tallcase clock as being hand finished with a hand-painted face, moving moon dial, and an eight-day, weight-driven triple-chime pendulum movement.

Century Furniture Company of Hickory, North Carolina, also contracted with the Henry Ford Museum in 1991 to produce pieces for the American Life Collec-

tion, including furniture for the bedroom and dining room, occasional and upholstered pieces made from cherry, mahogany, and pine. Promotional literature from Century details a Queen Anne-style highboy with cabriole legs, pinwheel carvings, and flame finials. Century also reproduces several rustic pieces and a few Federal era pieces.

In 1982 Winterthur Museum began a reproduction program with Kindel Furniture Company, copying some of the finest pieces in its collection, including the famous Goddard-Townsend secretary/bookcase from Newport, Rhode Island. Of the several made around 1760, one recently sold at auction for 12 million dollars! This obviously represents the height of eighteenth-century American design. The Kindel reproduction from the Winterthur Museum Collection is a hallmarked piece, copying the primary and secondary woods of the original, as well as many aspects of the original construction. Kindel also produces dining room furniture patterned after eighteenth and nineteenth-century American pieces at Winterthur. However, these pieces are not exact reproductions, but make accommodations to current customers' needs.

Kindel began making reproductions for the National Trust for Historic Preservation in 1984, based on originals from the various properties owned by the organization. In general, these tend to be more vernacular in style than the pieces reproduced for Winterthur.

The Society for the Preservation of New England Antiquities has had a reproduction program since 1983 in conjunction with Southwood Reproductions, Henkel-Harris Furniture Company, Frederick Duckloe and Bros., and Eldred Wheeler. These reproductions are all based on New England originals, from the many properties owned by the SPNEA. SPNEA materials from the 1980s show a Portsmouth, New Hampshire, Chippendale corner chair; a Maine blockfront chest of drawers; a Newport card table; a

c. 1735–1750 Massachusetts chest on frame; a Portsmouth Queen Anne dropleaf table by Henkle-Harris; a Boston comb-back Windsor chair by Duckloe and Bros.; a Boston easy chair with shell-carved knees and ball-and-claw feet; a Chippendale lolling chair; and a Federal sofa by Southwood Reproductions. Currently the firm of Eldred Wheeler makes a New Hampshire six-drawer chest on frame from the 1770s, and an eighteenth century oval-top tavern table from Portsmouth, New Hampshire.

Public interest in and support of these museums and their reproduction programs continues. With several new programs begun in the 1980s and 1990s, museums will probably provide a source of good quality Colonial reproductions for the foreseeable future. It will be interesting to see how these reproductions fare in the secondary market, particularly as we enter the twenty-first century, and twentieth-century reproductions become "antiques" in their own right. We suspect that museum-sponsored reproductions and the work of the smaller cabinetshops will be among the most sought-after reproductions.

BIBLIOGRAPHY

American Manufactured Furniture. West Chester, PA: Schiffer Publishing Ltd., 1988.

Ames, Kenneth L. "Grand Rapids Furniture at the Time of the Centennial." *Winterthur Portfolio* 10 (1975): 23–50.

Axelrod, Alan, ed. *The Colonial Revival in America.* New York: W. W. Norton, 1985.

Bainbridge, Bunting. *Houses of Boston's Back Bay.* Cambridge: The Belknap Press of Harvard University, 1975.

Bassett Furniture Industries. *A History of Bassett Furniture Industries, Inc.* Bassett, Virginia, c. 1985.

Betsky, Celia. "Inside the Past: The Interior and the Colonial Revival in American Art and Literature, 1860–1914." In Alan Axelrod, ed., *The Colonial Revival in America,* 241–77.

Burchell, Sam. *A History of Furniture— Celebrating Baker Furniture: One Hundred Years of Fine Reproductions.* New York: Harry N. Abrams, 1991.

Cook, Clarence. *The House Beautiful.* New York: Scribner, Armstrong and Company, 1878.

Cooke, Edward S. "The Boston Furniture Industry in 1880." *Old-Time New England* 70 (Winter 1980): 82–96.

Darling, Sharon. *Chicago Furniture: Art, Craft, and Industry, 1833–1983.* New York: W. W. Norton, 1984.

Dietz, Ulysses G. *Century of Revivals: Nineteenth-Century American Furniture from the Collection of the Newark Museum.* Newark NJ: Newark Museum of Art, 1983.

Ettema, Michael J. "Technological Innovation and Design Economics in Furniture Manufacture." *Winterthur Portfolio* 16 (Summer/Autumn 1981): 187–223.

Fennimore, Donald L. "Fine Points of Furniture, American Empire: Late, Later, Latest." In Kenneth L. Ames, *Victorian Furniture.* Philadelphia: The Victorian Society of America, 1983.

Hill, John H. "Furniture Designs of Henry W. Jenkins & Sons Co." *Winterthur Portfolio* (1969): 154–87.

The Housekeeper's Quest: Where to Find Pretty Things. New York: Sypher & Company, 1885.

Ingerman, Elizabeth. "Personal Experiences of an Old New York Cabinetmaker." *The Magazine Antiques* 84 (November 1963): 576–80.

Ivankovich, Michael. *The Guide to Wallace Nutting Furniture.* Doylestown, PA: Diamond Press, 1990.

Kimerly, W. L. *How to Know Period Styles in Furniture.* Grand Rapids, MI: Periodical Publishing Company, 1912.

Koch, Robert. *Louis C. Tiffany: Rebel in Glass.* Updated third edition. New York: Crown, 1982.

Lockwood, Luke Vincent. *Colonial Furniture in America.* New York: Scribner's, 1901.

Lyon, Irving Whitall. *Colonial Furniture of New England.* Boston and New York: Houghton Mifflin Company, 1891.

May, Bridget A. "Progressivism and the Colonial Revival: The Modern Colonial House, 1900–1920." *Winterthur Portfolio* 26 (Summer/Autumn 1991): 107–22.

McCabe, James D. *The Illustrated History of the Centennial Exhibition.* Philadelphia: National Publishing Company, 1876.

Monkhouse, Christopher P. "The Spinning Wheel as Artifact, Symbol, and Source of Design." In Kenneth Ames, ed., *Victorian Furniture,* Philadelphia: Victorian Society of America, 1983, 155–72.

Monkhouse, Christopher P., and Thomas S. Michie. *American Furniture in Pendleton House.* Providence: Museum of Art, Rhode Island School of Design, 1986.

Nutting, Wallace. *Wallace Nutting General Catalog, Supreme Edition.* 1930.

———. Wallace Nutting Windsors: Correct Windsor Furniture. Framingham, Mass: 1918.

———. *Wallace Nutting's Biography.* Framingham, Mass.: Old America Co., 1936.

Nye, Alvan Crocker. *A Collection of Scale-drawings, Details, and Sketches of what is commonly known as Colonial Furniture, Measured and drawn from antique examples by Alvan Crocker Nye.* New York: William Helburn, 1895.

Otto, Celia Jackson. *American Furniture of the Nineteenth Century.* New York: Viking Press, 1965.

Paine Furniture Company. "Suggestions to Those Who Would Furnish." Boston: 1888.

Pina, Leslie. *Louis Rorimer: A Man of Style.* Kent, Ohio: Kent State University Press, 1990.

Ransom, Frank Edward. *The City Built on Wood: A History of the Furniture Industry in Grand Rapids, Michigan, 1850–1950.* Ann Arbor, MI: Edwards Bros., 1955.

Rhoads, William B. *The Colonial Revival.* New York: Garland Publishing, 1977.

Roth, Rodris, "The Colonial Revival and Centennial Furniture." *Art Quarterly* 27, no. 1 (1964): 57–81.

———. "The New England, or 'Olde Tyme,' Kitchen Exhibit at Nineteenth-Century Fairs." In Alan Axelrod, ed., *The Colonial Revival in America,* 159–83.

Schoelwer, Susan Prendergast. "Curious Relics and Quaint Scenes: The Colonial Revival at Chicago's Great Fair." In Alan Axelrod, ed., *The Colonial Revival in America,* 185–216.

Seale, William. *The Tasteful Interlude: American Interiors Through the Camera's Eye, 1860–1917.* New York: Praeger Publishers, 1975.

Smith, Nancy A. *Old Furniture: Understanding the Craftsman's Art.* New York: Dover Publications, 1990.

Smith, Ray C. *Interior Design in Twentieth-Century America: A History.* New York: Harper and Row, 1987.

Stillinger, Elizabeth. *The Antiquers.* New York: Alfred A. Knopf, 1980.

Sypher & Company. "The Housekeeper's Quest: Where to Find Pretty Things." New York, 1885.

Thomas, David N. "A History of Southern Furniture." *Furniture South* 46, no. 10, sec. 2 (October 1967): 13–109.

Vollmer, William. *A Book of Distinctive Interiors.* New York: McBride, Nast, 1910.

Wallick, Ekin. *Inexpensive Furnishings in Good Taste.* New York: Hearst's International Library Company, 1915.

Weidman, Gregory R. *Furniture in Maryland, 1740–1940.* Baltimore: Maryland Historical Society, 1984.

LIST OF CONTRIBUTORS

Antiques Shops, Auction Houses, and Producers

Baker Furniture Company
1661 Monroe Ave. NW
Grand Rapids, Michigan 49505

Bassett Furniture Industries, Inc.
P.O. Box 626
Bassett, Virginia 24055

Frank H. Boos Gallery
420 Enterprise Court
Bloomfield Hills, Michigan 48301
(313) 332-1500

Butterfield & Butterfield
220 San Bruno Ave.
San Francisco, California 94103
(415) 861-7500

Century Furniture Company
P.O. Box 608
Hickory, NC 28603

Chameleon Antiques
10413 Warwick Blvd.
Newport News, Virginia 23601
(804) 596-9324

Chesapeake Antique Center, Inc.
Route 301
Queenstown, Maryland 21658
(410) 827-6640

William Doyle Galleries
175 East 87th Street
New York, New York 10128
(212) 427-2730

Dunning's Auction Service, Inc.
755 Church Road
Elgin, Illinois 60123
(708) 741-3483

Eldred Wheeler
60 Sharp Street
Hingham, Massachusetts 02043

Flomaton Antique Auction
207 Palafox Street
Flomaton, Alabama 36441
(205) 296-3710

Freeman/Fine Arts
1808–10 Chestnut Street
Philadelphia, Pennsylvania 19103
(215) 563-9275

Morton Goldberg Auction Galleries
547 Baronne Street
New Orleans, Louisiana 70113
(504) 592-2300

Grogan & Company
890 Commonwealth Avenue
Boston, Massachusetts 02215
(617) 566-4100

Henkle-Harris Furniture Company
P.O. Box 2170
Winchester, Virginia 22604

Leslie Hindman Auctioneers
215 West Ohio Street
Chicago, Illinois 60610
(312) 670-0010

Michael Ivankovich
P.O. Box 2458
Doylestown, Pennsylvania 18901
(215) 345-6094

James D. Julia, Inc.
Route 201, Showhegan Road
Fairfield, Maine 04937
(207) 453-7125

Kindel Furniture Company
P.O. Box 2047
Grand Rapids, Michigan 49501

Merriwood Antiques
3318 West Cary Street
Richmond, Virginia 23221
(804) 288-9308

Motley's Auction's, Inc.
2334 Willis Road
Richmond, Virginia 23237
(804) 743-8891

Nadeau's Auction Gallery
184 Windor Avenue
Windsor, Connecticut 06095
(203) 246-2444

Nansemond Antique Shop
3537 Pruden Boulevard
Suffolk, Virginia 23434
(804) 539-6269

Anthony J. Nard & Company
U.S. Route 220
Milan, Pennsylvania 18831
(717) 888-7723

Neal Auction Company
4038 Magazine Street
New Orleans, Louisiana 70115
(504) 899-5329

New Hampshire Antique Co-Op
Route 101A, Box 732
Milford, New Hampshire 03055

New Orleans Auction Galleries, Inc.
801 Magazine Street
New Orleans, Louisiana 70130
(504) 566-1849

Northeast Auctions
P.O. Box 363
Hampton, New Hampshire 03842
(603) 926-9800

Rafael Osona
P.O. Box 2607
Nantucket, Massachussets 02584
(508) 228-3942

Skinner, Inc.
Auctioneers and Appraisers of Antiques
    and Fine Art
357 Main Street
Bolton, Massachusetts 01740
(508) 779-6241

Sligh Furniture Company
201 W. Washington Avenue
Zeeland, Michigan 49464

C. G. Sloan & Company
4920 Wyaconda Road
North Bethesda, Maryland 20852
(401) 468-4911

Southampton Antiques
172 College Highway (Route 10)
Southampton, Massachusetts 01073
(413) 527-1022

Kimball M. Sterling, Inc.
125 West Market Street
Johnson City, Tennessee 37601
(615) 928-1471

Wolf's Fine Arts Auctioneers
1239 West 6th Street
Cleveland, Ohio 44113
(216) 575-9653

Museums and Libraries

Baker Furniture Library
1661 Monroe Avenue, Northwest
Grand Rapids, Michigan 49505

The Bennington Museum
West Main Street
Bennington, Vermont

The Colonial Williamsburg Foundation
P.O. Box 1776
Williamsburg, Virginia 23187

The Furniture Library
1009 North Main Street
High Point, North Carolina 27262

Grand Rapids Public Library
60 Library Plaza, Northeast
Grand Rapids, Michigan 49503

Henry Ford Museum
P.O. Box 1970
Dearborn, Michigan 48120

Edison Institute
20900 Oakwood Blvd.
Dearborn, Michigan 48121

International Home Furnishings Center
210 East Commerce Street
High Point, North Carolina 27260

Museum of Art
Rhode Island School of Design
Providence, Rhode Island 02903

Newark Museum
419 Washington Street
Newark, New Jersey 07101

Public Museum of Grand Rapids
54 Jefferson Southeast
Grand Rapids, Michigan 49503

Reynolda House
Museum of American Art
P.O. Box 11765
Winston-Salem, NC 27116

Smithsonian Institution
Washington, DC 20560

Society for the Preservation of New
    England Antiquities
141 Cambridge Street
Boston, Massachusetts 02114

The Winterthur Library
The Henry Frances du Pont Winterthur
    Museum
Winterthur, Delaware 19735

Index